LEGAL RECREATIONS.

VOL. IV.

THE LAW OF THE ROAD.

THE

LAW OF THE ROAD;

OR,

WRONGS AND RIGHTS OF A TRAVELLER.

BY

R. VASHON ROGERS, Jr.

A BARRISTER AT LAW OF OSGOODE HALL.

SAN FRANCISCO:
SUMNER WHITNEY AND COMPANY.
NEW YORK: HURD AND HOUGHTON.
Cambridge: The Riverside Press.

RIVERSIDE, CAMBRIDGE:
STEREOTYPED AND PRINTED BY
H. O. HOUGHTON AND COMPANY.

PREFACE

TO THE

CANADIAN EDITION.

THIS little work does not aspire to compete with the learned productions of Redfield, Chitty, or Story, but merely to supply a want, felt by many to exist in this age of perpetual motion, of a plain and brief summary of the rights and liabilities of carriers and passengers by land and by water.

An attempt is made in the following pages to combine instruction with entertainment, information with amusement, and to impart knowledge while beguiling a few hours in a railway carriage, or on a steamboat. Whilst it is hoped that the general public will peruse with interest the text, containing elegant extracts from ponderous legal tomes — gems from the rich mines of legal lore — and where in many cases the law is laid down in the very words of learned judges of England, Canada, and the United States; the notes — a cloud of authorities — the index and the list of cases are inserted for the special delectation of the professional reader.

Though written in Ontario, the book will be found applicable to all parts of the Dominion, as well as to the United States and England.

The author, even if the style is deemed novel, does not seek the praise of originality for the substance of the following chapters, as the greater portion of the text, and well nigh all the notes, have been taken from the works of others, to whom all due thanks are now rendered.

How far the book is likely to be of use to the seeker after knowledge, or of assistance to those desiring to kill time, is for others to determine. If mistakes be discovered it is hoped that the reader — professional or otherwise — will bear with them, "for if the work be found of sufficient merit to require another edition, they will probably be corrected, and if no such demand is made the book has received as much labor as it deserves."

The author is very "'umble, coming of an 'umble family," like the celebrated Uriah — not the Hittite, but he of the Heap tribe — and he will be quite content and satisfied if every reader, after having perused this work, says of him as Lord Thurlow said of Mansfield: "A surprising man; ninety-nine times out of a hundred he is right in his opinions and decisions, and when once in a hundred times he is wrong, ninety-nine men out of a hundred would not discover it."

PREFACE

TO THE

AMERICAN EDITION.

IN this present year of grace the British Lion is gently purring in the centennial eyry of the American Eagle; thither also, the Canadian Beaver, with a maple-leaf, the emblem of sweetness, in his mouth, has wended its way: a striking contrast to the deeds of one hundred years agone, when the followers of the quadrupeds were striving, teeth and claw, to send the lovers of the biped to that bourne from which no traveller returns.

The time seems therefore opportune for a member of the Beaver family to present to the worshippers of the mighty Eagle an edition of a little book touching upon the wrongs and the rights of those of the republic, and from distant lands, who travel upon the 74,000 miles traversed by the iron horse, or the hundreds of thousands of leagues frequented by nags of more mortal frame, on the American continent.

The following is a Canadian book, revised, enlarged, abridged (the watery element being omitted),[1] and rendered more suitable to the palate of Uncle Sam by the admixture of many more of the wise sayings of the men learned in the law of the United States. Originally published anonymously, the author has been induced, by the kind notices of his little book that have appeared, to acknowledge his bantling; and he would seize this opportunity of rendering thanks to those critics who, when writing of the first edition of his work, dipped their pens into a solution of sugar and honey and not into an extract of wormwood, vinegar and gall.

R. V. R. Jr.

Kingston, Ontario,
June, 1876.

[1] Also the List of Cases.

WRONGS AND RIGHTS OF A TRAVELLER.

CHAPTER I.

DRIVING.

New Year's Day. — Collision with Old Bolus. — Must I pay for my Servant's Deeds. — Deaf Man run over. — Effects of an Avalanche. — Housemaid injured by Coachman. — Wives, Snakes or Eels. — Icy Walks. — Falling Snow. — Board Walks. — Driver and driven. — Right Side or Wrong. — Look out. — Walkers. — Sunday Driving and Visiting. — Church-going. — Sunday Laws.

My life, so far as the readers of this sketch are concerned, may be taken to have commenced on the New Year's morning after I had married a wife, and set up a trap with the necessary accompaniments of a horse or two and a man.

It was my intention, pursuant to the time-honored custom, to go out in the afternoon with a friend to call upon my extensive circle of lady acquaintances. At 10 A. M. Mrs. Lawyer came into my library frantic and breathless; the palpitations of her heart having somewhat subsided, and her heaving bosom sunk to rest, she exclaimed: —

"O Eldon, that horrid John must be drunk! He took out the horse and sleigh this morning, and when driving down Main Street, he ran into Dr. Bolus's cutter and knocked it all to pieces."

"Ah, my dear Elizabeth, calm your troubled mind;" I coolly replied, "John, without my knowledge, and wrongfully, took my horse and sleigh for some purpose or other of his own, and ran into old Bolus's turn-out, you say: well, the law is perfectly clear that I am not responsible for the injury, as I did not intrust my servant with the sleigh.[1] I may tell you for your edification that the general rule is that a master is not liable for the tortious act of his servant, unless that act be done by an authority, either express or implied, given him for that purpose by the master;[2] or as Mr. Baron Parke puts it, if a servant is going on a frolic of his own, without being at all on his master's business, the master will not be liable."[3]

"Oh, but dear Don, I forgot to tell you that I sent him to the confectioner's for some cakes; but I told him to drive along West Street."

"Confound it, that 's a different matter. The Doctor will rush off to friend Erskine, and I will have to pony up for the damage; because, as that rascal John was driving on his master's business,

[1] M'Manus *v.* Crickett, 1 East, 106; Croft *v.* Alison, 4 B. & Ald. 590; Sleath *v.* Wilson, 9 C. & P. 607, qualified by Seymour *v.* Greenwood, 6 H. & N. 359, 7 H. & N. 355; Lamb *v.* Palk, 9 C. & P. 631; Sheridan *v.* Charlick, 4 Daly, 338.

[2] Roe *v.* Birkenhead, etc., Rw. Co., 7 Ex. 36.

[3] Joel *v.* Morison, 6 C. & P. 501.

it matters not that he disobeyed his express orders in going out of his way, or made a detour to please himself."[1]

"Yes, but Eldon dear," continued my wife, "it was not on his master's business, it was on mine."

"Stupid, what difference does that make?" replied I, impatiently; and then, seeing that my wife did not like the adjective, I added more feelingly, but rather vaguely, "Don't you see, I'm his master, you are mine, and so must be his also."

"Heigh-ho!" sighed the wife of my bosom. "But I have not told you all. After the collision the horse ran against an old man who was walking along the street, knocked him down, and hurt him: but, of course, he had no right to be on the road, when there was a good sidewalk for him."

"Of course he *had* a right to be on the road, just as much right there as the horse and sleigh had, even though he were sick and infirm; and it was John's business to take care where he was going!"[2]

"Yet John says he told the man to get out of the way, and he would n't do it;" pleaded my wife.

[1] Limpus *v.* London Omn. Co., 1 H. & C. 526; Joel *v.* Morison, 6 C. & P. 501; Mitchell *v.* Crassweller, 13 C. B. 237; Seymour *v.* Greenwood, 7 H. & N. 356.

[2] Boss *v.* Litton, 5 C. & P. 407; Brooks *v.* Schwerin, 54 N. Y. 343.

"That does not matter.[1] I hope no more damage was done?" I queried.

"Yes; the horse shied and upset the sleigh; and John says that all his — I mean John's — ribs are broken, and that he is kilt entirely; and he swears that he 'll make you pay for it — that he 'll sue you."

"Let him sue away and be hanged; he 'll get nothing for his pains but the pleasure of spending his earnings; he is my servant and has to run the risk of being hurt in my employment."[2]

"But then, Eliza Jane, the housemaid, was with him, was thrown out too, and had all the skin taken off her face; and she says she 'll sue too."

"Oh, I 'm sorry for that; I like her, and then she was so pretty."

"Eldon! how dare you say so — to your wife, too!"

"I — I — only meant that I would have to pay for the damage to her, and that if I did not do it willingly, any jury would be persuaded by her pretty face to give a heavy sum against me for the injury done to her by my servant.[3] Well, 't is a pretty how-do-ye-do for a New Year's gift. I 'll go down and see the wretch."

Off I went, glad to get out of Elizabeth's sight.

[1] Woolley *v.* Scovell, 3 M. & Ry. 105.

[2] Paterson *v.* Wallace, 1 Macq. 751; Meara's Admr. *v.* Holbrook, 20 Ohio St. 137; C. & A. R. R. Co. *v.* Murphy, 53 Ill. 339.

[3] Lord Cranworth, Bartonshill Coal Co. *v.* Reid, 3 Macq. 294-307.

She had grown a little jealous because I had shown a few trifling civilities to pretty Eliza Jane, — very trifling they were, I assure you; besides I wanted to vent my rage on the man John. In a very short time some words and phrases were used in the yard to which, doubtless, Moses would have objected, if he had the first table of stone in his hand. My ire, however, cooled down in time when I found that the man was "all serene," and that all the trouble had been caused by the horse having taken fright at the fall of a lot of snow and ice off a house-top — a circumstance over which, of course, I had not the slightest control; and therefore I was not liable to Dr. Bolus, the old man, nor to pretty Eliza Jane.[1] But to make matters all straight I gave my man a couple of dollars, and meeting E. J. on the back-stairs as I went in I chucked her under her dimpled chin, and told her that crying would make her pretty eyes look red and swollen; and then retiring to my library read up all the cases bearing on the subject, beginning with the old case of Michael *v.* Alistree,[2] where the defendants "in Lincoln's Inn Fields, a place where people are always going to and fro about their business, brought a coach with two ungovernable horses, *et ex improvide, incaute et absque consideratione inaptitudinis loci*, there

[1] Wakeman *v.* Robinson, 1 Bing. 213; Hammack *v.* White, 11 C. B. (N. S.) 588; Gibbons *v.* Pepper, 1 Ld. Raym. 38; Jackson *v.* Bellevieu, 30 Wis. 257; Livingston *v.* Adams, 8 Cow. 175; Ficken *v.* Jones, 28 Cal. 618.

[2] 2 Lev. 172; 1 Ventr. 295.

drove them, etc., and the horses, because of their ferocity, being not to be managed, ran into the plaintiff, and hurt and grievously wounded him," and the plaintiff got damages as well as damaged.

At the appointed hour my friend and young brother-in-the-law, Tom Jones, arrived. As he sank into one of the softest of our drawing-room chairs, and gazed around, he exclaimed: —

"By Jove, Eldon, you look so snug and cosy here that I am half inclined to follow suit, quit our bachelor's hall, marry a nice little girl I wot of, and settle down."

"Do so at once," said my wife.

"Ah! I cannot forget the words of that good old judge, Sir John Moore," he replied with a sigh.

"Oh, you are as bad as Eldon, always quoting some fusty old judge. But what did he say?" queried my wife.

"He said that he would compare the multitude of women who are to be chosen for wives unto a bag full of snakes, having among them a single eel. Now, if a man should put his hand into this bag, he might chance to light on the eel, but it is one hundred to one he would be stung by a snake," returned Jones.

"The horrid old wretch. I am sure I was neither a snake nor an eel: was I, Eldon? I hate both."

"Oh, no, my dear," I replied. "But Tom,

that surely is only an *obiter dictum*, not a decision of that worthy judge."

"Of course," replied Jones; "but all the dicta of judges are entitled to weight." Tom had just been called to the bar.

"It is time that you two horrid creatures left here," said Mrs. L.

"Well, suppose we start. Mind dear, to tell the man to be sure to meet us, two hours from now, at Mrs. Smith's."

"Is your life insured against accidents, Mr. Jones?" asked my wife. "You are sure to be run away with and upset."

"Only against railway accidents," he said.

"That 's stupid," I remarked, "for it is well settled that hardly seven per cent. of accidental claims arise from accidents in travelling by rail or water, while those arising from horse or carriage injuries exceed in number those from all other causes combined."

"A pleasant idea wherewith to start for an afternoon's drive," quoth Tom.

Off we went, followed by the best wishes of my loving and lovely spouse. Scarce had our feet touched the sidewalk when, with the exclamation, "Get out you rascallion!" Jones executed a *pas seul*, and then lay sprawling on the ground; and the small boy — whose sled as it slid swiftly down the board walk my friend had vainly endeavored to avoid — glided merrily on. As I whisked the snow off, Jones in wrathful accents consigned the juvenile to a place beyond the possible limits of frost, and exclaimed: —

"I'll sue the city for allowing the road to be in such a beastly state. Corporations are bound to keep the street in a proper condition, so that the lives and bones of passers-by will not be endangered."

"True," I replied, "but the accident was not wholly caused by the slipperiness of the pavement; the unlawful and careless act of the boy in coasting had something to do with your overthrow; and in the exactly similar case of Mrs. Shepherd it was decided that the city was not liable." [1]

"I tell you all towns and cities must keep their highways and streets in repair, so that they are without obstructions or structural defects which may endanger the safety of travellers, and are sufficiently level and smooth, and guarded by railings when necessary, to enable people, by the exercise of ordinary care, to move about with safety and convenience." [2]

"You repeated that sentence very well and with great emphasis. It is quite correct in a general way that highways, streets and sidewalks should at all times be safe and convenient, but

[1] Shepherd *et ux.* *v.* Chelsea, 4 Allen, 113; Hutchinson *v.* Concord, 41 Vt. 271; Ray *v.* Manchester, 46 N. H. 59.

[2] Hixon *v.* Lowell, 13 Gray, 59; Barber *v.* Roxbury, 11 Allen, 320; Hewison *v.* New Haven, 34 Conn. 142.

then regard must be had to the locality and intended uses.[1] Towns are liable only for injuries caused by defects and obstructions for which they might be indicted.[2] They do not insure the safety of all using sidewalks in the depths of our northern winters;[3] and it has been expressly decided that the mere existence of a little ice on the walk is no evidence of actionable negligence:[4] the slipperiness of the ice, if the walk is properly constructed and free from accumulations of snow, will not give those who fall a right to sue a city with success.[5] One must go gingerly and with due care on such occasions."[6]

"All very fine," said Jones, "but when my friend Clapp, in walking along the streets of the city of Providence, at night, fell on some ice and broke his thigh, he recovered damages."

"Yes, I remember; but then there was a ridge of ice and snow, hard trodden, in the centre of the sidewalk, which was considered such an obstacle as the city should have removed.[7] And" —

Ere I had completed my sentence the hour of my doom had struck, and I was as white as ever miller was; an avalanche of snow slid off a roof and thundered down on my devoted head. Jones

1 City of Providence *v.* Clapp, 17 How. 168.

2 Merrill *v.* Hampden, 26 Me. 234.

3 Ringland *v.* Toronto, 23 C. P. Ont. 93.

4 Ibid.

5 Stanton *v.* Springfield, 12 Allen, 566; Hutchins *v.* Boston, Ib. 571 n.

6 Wilson *v.* Charlestown, 8 Allen, 137.

7 City of Providence *v.* Clapp, 17 How. 168; Church *v.* Cherryfield, 33 Me 460.

with a smirk asked me if I was going to sue for damages. Sadly, as I twisted my head slowly round and nodded first to right and then to left, to see if the vertebræ were all in working order, I replied: —

"Ah, no! I cannot do so with success.[1] It 's a case of *damnum absque injuria.*"

"Ho! ho!" laughed my companion; "strong language; but no wonder."

"If the owner of the house had left the ice and snow there for an unusual and unreasonable time after he knew of its presence and might have removed it, he probably would have been liable to me,[2] or, if that old awning had fallen on me,[3] or if that lamp hanging over the Sol's Arms' door had lighted on my crown, producing an extra bump, for the edification of Fowler and Wells and the savants of that ilk, I might have got something in the first case out of the city; in the other from the landlord.[4] Or if one of those barrels had rolled out of that warehouse, and, thumping against your legs, had brought you down, you might have sued the merchant."[5]

"Look at that poor old woman; she will come to grief most assuredly."

Before us toddled an aged granny, assisting her

1 Hixon *v.* Lowell, 13 Gray, 59.
2 Shipley *v.* Fifty Associates, 101 Mass. 251; *S. C.* 106 Mass. 194.
3 Drake *v.* Lowell, 13 Met. 292.
4 Tarry *v.* Ashton, L. R., 1 Q. B. D. 314.
5 Byrne *v.* Boadle, 2 H. & C. 722; Randleson *v.* Murray, 8 Ad. & E. 109.

septuagenarian extremities with an antique looking umbrella, of no color known to this life. It was of a "flabby habit of waist, and seemed to be in need of stays, looking as if it had served the old dame for long years as a cupboard at home, as a carpet-bag abroad."

"So feeble a person should not be out in such slippery weather unattended;[1] people should exercise common prudence. One who has poor sight should take greater care in walking the streets than one in full enjoyment of her faculties."[2]

"I fancy the least obstacle or hole would upset her," said Tom.

"And if she did stumble over a small impediment she could not sue the city for damages. So the court held where a man fell over the hinge of a trap-door projecting a couple of inches above the sidewalk in a village.[3] But the degree of repair in which the walks must be kept depends considerably upon the locality; one may reasonably expect better pavements in a city than in a village; and so in Boston where an iron box four inches square, set in a sidewalk by a gas company, had a rim projecting an inch above the level, the city was held responsible for injuries caused by it."[4]

"If she did meet with an accident and was held entitled to damage, what would she get in hard cash?" asked Jones.

[1] Davenport *v.* Ruckman, 37 N. Y. 568.
[2] Winn *v.* Lowell, 1 Allen, 180.
[3] Ray *v.* Petrolia, 24 C. P. Ont. 73.
[4] Loan *v.* Boston, 106 Mass. 450; Bacon *v.* Boston, 3 Cush. 174.

" 'Tis impossible to say. It would depend upon so many things. In one case where an old man of seventy, who was very feeble, fell at night into an opening for a drain in the sidewalk, which was covered with boards laid at right angles with the others and projecting some two inches, over which he stumbled, the jury gave $4,000 damages; but the court held that excessive, as the old man was insolvent and incapable of much labor."[1]

" That was a large sum for injuries."

" But the old fellow died. We go in here," I added.

" You may, I will not," replied Jones, as he leant against the railing of a bridge over a little stream.

" Well, do not stand there; if the board gives way and lets you down, you will have no remedy against the city; for it is not bound to keep up railings strong enough for idlers to lounge against, or children to play upon.[2] Look out, there is another sled!" As I rang the door-bell I heard Jones mutter: —

" Those boys ought to be indicted for obstructing the sidewalk in such a way."

" True for you," I mentally ejaculated, " I remember that one of those bewitched and besaddled wheelbarrow concerns, yclept velocipedes, was held to be an indictable obstruction."[3]

[1] Hutton *v.* Windsor, 34 Q. B. Ont. 487.

[2] Stickney *v.* Salem, 3 Allen, 374; Gregory *v.* Adams, 14 Gray, 242.

[3] Reg. *v.* Plummer, 30 Q. B. Ont. 41.

In due time my servant met us with the sleigh, and off we went, bells jingling, horse prancing, dog barking, all joyous with the exhilarating influences of frost and sunshine.

"Look here, old fellow," said Tom, "your horse seems pretty skittish to-day; let us settle the law as to our mutual liability for damages before we run into anything. Who will have to pay? You don't seem very much accustomed to driving."

"Never mind that. The law is clear; as you are merely a passenger in my sleigh, you are not responsible for any misconduct of which I may be guilty while driving; you have nothing to do with the concern.[1] Even if I had only borrowed the turn-out, and kindly let you take the ribbons, I still would be the party responsible for negligence."[2]

"That 's satisfactory," returned my friend. "But would it not be different if we had both hired the horse and cutter?"

"Quite correct, Mr. T. J.; your store of legal lore is rapidly accumulating. In the case you put, both of us would be equally answerable for any accident arising from the misconduct of either whilst it was under our joint care,[3] and if we had hired the horses to draw my sleigh, and had likewise obtained the services of a driver, then we

1 Davey *v.* Chamberlain, 4 Esp. 229.
2 Wheatley *v.* Patrick, 2 M. & W. 650.
3 Davey *v.* Chamberlain, 4 Esp. 229.

would not be liable for the negligence or carelessness of that driver."[1]

"Look out! you had better keep on your own side of the road," said Jones.

"Never mind, I can go on either side. I 'll only have to keep my eye a little wider open to avoid collisions;[2] besides, there is plenty of room for any person to pass, so he would have only himself to blame in case of accidents."[3]

"A person approaching you might think there was not sufficient space."

"If an accident happens, it will be a matter of evidence whether I have left ample room or not;[4] so you can look about you and see."

"But suppose some fiery steed was to run into yours?" urged Thomas, "or you upset in the ditch?"

"My being on the wrong side would not prevent my recovering against a negligent driver, as long as there is room for him to pass without inconvenience.[5] Nor would it interfere with my getting damages from the city for injuries caused by their defective roads.[6] Whoa, old fellow!" I cried, just as I was on the point of running over a philosopher who was walking slowly over a

1 Laugher *v.* Pointer, 5 B. & C. 547; Quarman *v.* Burnett, 6 M. & W. 499.
2 Pluckwell *v.* Wilson, 5 C. & P. 375.
3 Chaplin *v.* Hawes, 3 C. & P. 554.
4 Wordsworth *v.* Willan, 5 Esp. 273.
5 Clay *v.* Wood, 5 Esp. 44.
6 Baker *v.* Portland, 10 Am. Law Reg. (N. S.), 559, 58 Me. 199; Gale *v.* Lisbon, 52 N. H. 174.

crossing gazing up at the azure vault of heaven. "What a stupid donkey; it is as much his business to be watchful and cautious that he does not get under my sleigh, as it is mine that my sleigh does not get over him![1] It is gross carelessness for one to attempt to cross a street when he sees a horse and vehicle coming rapidly along; and if that fellow had been injured, he could have got nothing out of me.[2] A man who does not use all his senses when crossing a highway is guilty of contributory negligence, and so loses all right of action."[3]

"Yes," said T. J. "Still a foot passenger has a clear right to cross a road, and persons driving must avoid running him down; it will be no valid excuse that one could not pull up his nag for fear of the reins breaking, for he should have good harness.[4] But we may pass a pedestrian promenading on the road on whichever side is most convenient, for the rules of the road do not apply to walkers;[5] they have no prior right of way."[6]

"No; men walking and driving have equal rights on the streets; all must exercise care and prudence;[7] and a pedestrian should not indulge in nice calculations of chances, and run the gauntlet of carriages in crossing a road."[8]

1 Williams *v.* Richards, 3 C. & K. 81.

2 Woolf *v.* Beard, 8 Car. & P. 373.

3 Gray *v.* Second Avenue R. R. Co., 34 N. Y. Sup. Ct. (2 Jones & Spencer), 519.

4 Cotterill *v.* Starkey, 8 C. & P. 691.

5 Cotterill *v.* Starkey, *supra*; Lloyd *v.* Ogleby, 5 C. B. (N. S.), 667.

6 Belton *v.* Baxter, 14 Abb. (N. Y.) Pr. (N. S.) 404.

7 Brooks *v.* Schwerin, 54 N. Y. 343.

8 Belton *v.* Baxter, *supra*

"I was out driving last Sunday" — Jones began.

"Oh, you naughty man!" I cried. "Have you no respect for the Sabbath day? or perhaps you wanted to have a ride without giving a *quid pro quo?*"

"How could I do that?" queried my friend.

"Don't you know," replied I, "that a man cannot recover for the hire of a horse and buggy, let on Sunday for a pleasure drive?[1] But if the livery man imagined that the errand on which you were bound was one of necessity or charity, he would not be punishable for a breach of the Sunday laws."[2]

"Well, but my drive was a work of charity (according to its original meaning), if not of necessity. I was going to see Miss Blank."

"That very point was raised sometime since in Massachusetts, where travelling on the Lord's Day is forbidden. A young man, who had to work all the week, was going to visit his betrothed on Sunday, when he came to grief through a defect in the highway. The question whether this might not have been a work of necessity or charity, was raised, but unfortunately, the matter was not decided.[3] In one case, however, it was held that a man might lawfully hire a horse and carriage to go and visit his paternal progenitor,

[1] Berrill *v.* Smith, 2 Miles, 402.
[2] Myers *v.* The State, 1 Conn. 502.
[3] Buffinton *v.* Swansey, 2 Am. Law Rev. 235.

who resided in the country.[1] In some of the States, where the laws for the observance of the Sabbath are rigorous, and travelling on that day is forbidden, young swells hire horses and race them, knowing that they will not have to pay for any injuries done to the old nags;[2] not even if they die from the Jehu-like driving.[3] But, come, let us hear more about Miss Blank, Joney, my boy."

"I presume," said Jones, "that one hurt while travelling would have to show that the journey was from necessity or charity? Would one have to stay in the house all day?"

"Oh, no; even in Puritanic Boston it has been decided that walking half a mile or so in the streets on a Sunday evening, without any intention of going anywhere save home again, is not travelling within the meaning of the act.[4] And of course one may go to church or to his place of worship, no matter what may be the style of the ceremony. Once Mrs. Feital, a Spiritualist, went to a camp-meeting where Miss Ellis was put in a box with her hands tied: music was heard coming from the box, and when it was open Miss Ellis was found with her hands untied, and a ring that had been on her finger was then on the end of her nose. On her way home from these amusing, if

1 Logan *v.* Mathews, 6 Penn. St. 417.
2 Gregg *v.* Wyman, 4 Cush. 322; but see Hall *v.* Corcoran, 107 Mass. 251.
3 Morton *v.* Gloster, 46 Me. 520.
4 Hamilton *v.* Boston, 14 Allen, 475.

not instructive services, Mrs. Feital broke her leg on the cars. The railway company tried to prove that this was not divine service, but the jury gave a verdict of $5,000 damages, and the court refused to interfere.[1] On the other hand, a poor sinner who was injured on a horse car while going to visit a friend, was held to have violated the sanctity of the Sabbath and broken the law of the land, and so was precluded from recovering damages."[2]

"But is not the rule in Massachusetts exceptional?" queried my companion.

"In Vermont and Maine, as well as in Massachusetts, it has been held that if one is driving or travelling on Sunday, without excuse, he cannot maintain an action against the municipality for any damage he may suffer through defects in the highway, on the ground that the town is not legally liable to furnish a man with a safe highway at a time when he is by law forbidden to travel on it.[3] Some of the decisions in these States depend upon the peculiar legislation and custom of the State, more than on any principle of justice or law;[4] and they cannot be sustained consistently with the broad principles of the law

1 Feital *v.* Middlesex R. R. Co., 109 Mass. 398.

2 Stanton *v.* Metropolitan Rw., 2 Am. Law Rev. 234.

3 Johnson *v.* Warburgh, 14 Am. Law Reg. 547; Jones *v.* Andover, 10 Allen, 18; Bosworth *v.* Swansey, 10 Met. 363; Hinckley *v.* Penobscot, 42 Me. 89; Bryant *v.* Biddeford, 59 Me. 193.

4 Per Grier, J. Phil., etc., R. R. Co. *v.* Phil., etc., Towboat Co., 23 How 209.

of negligence laid down by the courts generally.[1] The fact that one was doing an unlawful act when injured will not prevent a recovery, unless the act was such as would naturally tend to produce the injury.[2] If one breaks the law, the law itself, and not a carrier or town, should inflict the penalty. In other States, — New Hampshire, New York, Pennsylvania, Wisconsin, for example, one can sue for damages though injured while travelling on Sunday.[3] And in England Sunday travellers are especially favored by the legislature, for to none others can the publican dispose of beer, wine or spirits on that day.[4] But come, what about Miss Blank ?"

"By the way," said Jones, "have you seen that anecdote told by Erskine about Lord Kenyon, and which has recently been brought to light ?"

"No. Has it anything to do with driving ?"

"Everything. Kenyon was trying a case at the Guildhall and seemed disposed to leave it to the jury to say whether the plaintiff might not have saved himself from being run into by the defendant by going on to the wrong side of the road, where — according to the witnesses — was ample room ; so Lord Erskine in addressing the jury

1 Wharton on Negligence, § 405.

2 Wharton on Negligence, § 331, and cases cited.

3 Sutton v. Wauwantosa, 29 Wis. 21 ; Dutton v. Weare, 17 N. H. 34 ; Mohney v. Cook, 26 Pa. St. 342 ; Etchberry v. Levielle, 2 Hilton (N. Y.), 40.

4 Byles, J. Taylor v. Humphreys, 10 C B. (N. S.), 429.

said: 'Gentlemen,—If the noble and learned judge, in giving you hereafter his advice, shall depart from the only principle of safety (unless where collisions are selfish and malicious), and you shall act upon it, I can only say that I shall feel the same confidence in his lordship's general learning and justice, and shall continue to delight, as I always do, in attending his administration of justice: *but I pray God that I may never meet him on the road!'* Lord Kenyon laughed, and so did the jury, and in summing up the judge told them that he believed it to be the best course *stare super antiquas vias.*"

"Not so bad!"

On and on we drove; the very air seemed alive with the tintinnabulation that so musically wells from the jingling and the tinkling of the bells in the icy air of winter.

CHAPTER II.

A SLEIGH DRIVE.

Fast Driving.— Teams passing.— Clearing Snow.— Impassable Roads. — Stuck in a Snow-drift.— Upset.— Demolishing Juveniles. — Mind your Children. — In the Ditch. — Damages for Bad Roads. — Unsafe Bridges. — Horses shying. — Whisking Tails. — Runaways.

ALL the morning

> "Out of the bosom of the air,
> Out of the cloud-folds of her garments shaken,
> Over the woodlands brown and bare,
> Over the harvest fields forsaken,
> Silent, and soft, and slow,
> Descended the snow,"

But when the sun turned downwards towards his couch, he shone out clear and bright, making every snow-flake glisten and sparkle in the bracing air; so Mrs. L. determined to utilize the splendid weather, and pay a round of country visits. Of course I had to drive her.

The steeds needed no whip to urge them on. Swiftly we glided down the street, and over the bridge we trotted fast without drawing rein. The boards creaked and cracked, as when one strives to creep upstairs, unheard, at midnight. My wife said in surprise: —

"Eldon, did you not observe the notice threatening prosecution according to the utmost rigor of the law to all crossing the bridge quicker than at a walk? Why do lawyers break the law?"

"All right, my dear; if the bridge had broken down while we were trotting over it, I could not have sued the owners for damages.[1] But as we are over it, we need not discuss the subject."

"But," urged my wife, "it is not right to drive so fast."

"No; I know it. In fact it is an indictable offense to drive through crowded streets like these so as to endanger the safety of others." [2]

"How fast may one go?"

"That is difficult to say. Depends on circumstances. A mile in four minutes is too fast;[3] and if you go a mile in three minutes and ten seconds you become liable for all consequences.[4] Even where a man was driving at only a smartish pace and ran over a donkey he had to pay for it.[5] But one may drive rapidly on an open country road where the chance of collision is slight."

"Look out, Eldon!" cried my gentle spouse. "See, a load of wood has just upset there! What a nuisance!"

"Not legally so, as the man went over accidentally." [6]

1 Abbott *v.* Wolcott, 38 Vt. 666.
2 U. S. *v.* Hart, Peters C. C. 390.
3 Kennedy *v.* Way, 8 Law Reporter (N. S.), 184, Brightley (Pa.), 186.
4 Moody *v.* Osgood, 60 Barb. 644.
5 Davies *v.* Mann, 10 M. & W. 545.
6 Angell on Highways, § 263.

As we drove past we heard the woodman complaining bitterly that a sleigh that had just met him had not turned out enough, and hence his mishap.

"Too bad," I said; "people ought to show an accommodating spirit and cautious watchfulness in avoiding difficulties when the roads are so badly blocked with snow."[1]

"But," said my wife, who seemed to have an idea in her head, — there was an abundance of room for it, — of qualifying herself to carry on my business if some unforeseen event should chance to carry me off before I had realized some little independence. "But, I thought the towns, or corporations, were bound to keep their roads safe and convenient. I am sure that this one is neither safe nor convenient when we have to pass any one."

"Your supposition is correct. The rule applies as well to a turnpike company as to a town,[2] and to defects and obstructions caused by drifts of snow.[3] Accumulations of snow and ice must be removed so that streets and highways may be passable.[4] Of course it is plain, as a Canadian judge once remarked, that the owner of a road cannot be expected to clear the snow off the ground whenever it falls, or even to remove the

[1] Hull *v.* Richmond, 2 Wood. & M. 343.

[2] Mathews *v.* Winooski Turnpike Co., 24 Vt. 480.

[3] Loker *v* Brookline, 13 Pick. 346; Holman *v.* Townsend, 13 Met. 297.

[4] City of Providence *v.* Clapp, 17 How. 168.

ice which may form there. It would frequently be an impossible work to attempt it, and it would often be mischievous and a nuisance to effect it. Snow forms the best and most suitable means of travel in winter, and even when it falls to a great and unusual depth, it is not the duty of any one, as a rule, to remove it from the road. Nor can any one be required to remove mud and mire from a road. There are, however, cases when snow, ice, and mud may and must be removed, and that is when they cause an obstruction or danger which can properly and reasonably be removed.[1]

"If the corporation neglects its duty, what must an unfortunate traveller do?"

"If the highway is impassable for any reason, he certainly should not try to force a passage, for he would not be able to recover for his loss of time, or his trouble and expense in extricating his team from a snow-drift.[2] But he may go upon the adjoining land,[3] as we are going to do now."

"That is rather hard upon the poor farmers," said my wife. "Why, we may be driving over a field of fall wheat!"

"That makes no difference; one ought, however, to keep as near the road as possible."[4]

"It takes much longer going by this circuitous

[1] Wilson, J. Caswell *v.* St. Mary's, etc., Road Co., 28 Q. B. (Ont.), 247.

[2] Brailey *v.* Southborough, 6 Cush. 141; Willard *v.* Cambridge, 3 Allen, 574. In Massachusetts one cannot recover damages for not being able to use the road, though he may for injuries received while using it.

[3] Woolrych on Ways (2d ed.), 78; Campbell *v.* Race, 7 Cush. 408.

[4] Taylor *v.* Whitehead, 2 Dougl. 749; Carrick *v.* Johnston, 26 Q. B. (Ont.), 65.

route," said Mrs. Lawyer, with a woman's impatience.

"Still, unfortunately, we cannot get compensation from the town for the delay, even though we had to neglect important business in consequence.[1] But if, in addition to being made to neglect business, one, after commencing his journey, is obliged to turn back and go by a very roundabout way, there is some authority to show that he may get damages."[2]

For some minutes we had been winding in and out among lofty pines and evergreens with boughs weighed down by the snow upon them, which was now succumbing to the warm rays of the sun. Something caused my horses to shy suddenly, and over we went, cutter, wife, buffaloes, self, and all. Fortunately our steeds did not run off. At first, when I saw my spouse lying extended on the ground, I was alarmed, but she quickly reassured me by exclaiming: —

"Pleasant it is, when woods are green,
And winds are soft and low,
To lie amid some sylvan scene,
Where, the long drooping boughs between,
Shadows dark and sunlight sheen,
Alternate come and go.

"Beneath some patriarchal tree
I lie upon the 'snaw,'
His hoary arm uplifted he,
And all the white leaves over me
Dripping their little drops in glee,
In one continuous thaw."

[1] Hubert *v.* Groves, 1 Esp. 148; Griffin *v.* Sanbornton, 44 N. H. 246.
[2] Greasley *v.* Codling, 2 Bing. 263.

"Come, come, get up," I said. "Don't lie there playing the improvisatore and taking your death of cold, for I fear me I could not recover damages, although we had to come in here because the road was impassable, as I knew it was so before I set out, and therefore ought to have gone some other way and not have come into this bush at my peril."[1]

Soon all was again as it had been, and merrily onward we went, now and then calling at a house for a few minutes, and then on and on and on. The day was too gloriously bright to spend much time with our friends talking scandal. We came upon some children engaged in the exhilarating amusement of sliding down hill, and one of them we nearly annihilated. The horses' feet were well nigh upon him before we noticed his little red brick-top standing out in bold relief against the pure white snow.

"Ha!" I said, with a sigh of relief, "'t is well we did not knock the youngster into a cocked hat. It might have taken a good slice off my year's profits if I had. I remember a man who was driving a loaded team down a hill at no snail's pace, when he came upon a little rascal (not four years old) on his way to school, and who — to relieve the monotony of the journey — was sliding down the hill (near the edge of the road) lying upon his potatoe pouch on his hand-sleigh, his face turned towards the right, his legs Y-like

[1] Tisdale v. Norton, 8 Met. 388.

stretching out behind in the opposite direction. At a distance the man had taken the boy for a dog, then as he came nearer he thought the child would get out of the way, and when at length he did himself try to turn out, — although there was plenty of room, — still the hind runners injured the boy's left leg so much that amputation was necessary. The man had to pay heavy damages for the injuries he had inflicted."[1]

"It seems hard that one should have to pay for a parent's negligence in allowing such infants to wander about by themselves," said Mrs. L.

"Occasionally the tables are turned. Mr. Roper was once driving in his sleigh at a gentle trot (there were some of his family with him and strange to say they were not talking), when at the foot of a hill they ran over a baby two years old that was sitting in the snow in the middle of the road all by himself. The jury gave the child a verdict of $500, but the court would not hear of such a thing, considering that the parents had been guilty of criminal negligence in suffering the child to be in such a place."[2]

"I guess that court was composed of old bachelors," exclaimed my wife in indignant accents.

"Well, my dear, even married judges, and those who have been blessed with quivers full of those sharp things, children, have declared the rule to

[1] Robinson *v.* Cone, 3 Law Reporter (N. S.), 444; 22 Vt. 213.
[2] Hartfield *v.* Roper 21 Wend. 615; but see *post.*

be that, if the plaintiff's negligence in any way concurred in causing the damage, he cannot recover unless he could not, by the exercise of ordinary care, have avoided the injury, or the defendant has been guilty of gross negligence, or intentionally did the wrong." [1]

A little feminine chit-chat now occupied our attention; criticism concerning the friends we had been visiting, their foibles and weaknesses; speculations as to the incomes of the husbands, the age of the wives, and such like remarks which absorb such a large proportion of the atmospheric air that is converted into language.

In passing a man, he would not turn out, and I grazed his horses' legs, causing the animals to plunge and kick so as to knock the cutter about considerably; but seeing that the fellow was drunk and not able to drive properly, I was not at all alarmed about any damage I might have done, for I knew that I could not be held responsible.[2]

The sun had gone to rest; the stars were coming out one by one, dotting the vault of heaven as with sparkling gems. We heard in the distance the ringing laughter and the tinkling bells of a merry driving party. My wife exclaimed: —

> "Hear the sledges with the bells,
> Silver bells!
> What a world of merriment their melody foretells!

1 Barnes *v.* Cole, 21 Wend. 188; Bridge *v.* Grand Junction Rw., 3 M. & W 246.

2 Cassedy *v.* Stockbridge, 21 Vt. 391.

How they tinkle, tinkle, tinkle,
In the icy air of night!
While the stars that oversprinkle
All the heavens, seem to twinkle
With a crystalline delight:
Keeping time, time, time,
In a sort of Runic rhyme,
To the tintinabulation that so musically wells
From the bells, bells, bells, bells,
Bells, bells, bells —
From the jingling and the tinkling of the bells."

We were at this time driving down in a ditch for the sake of the snow (the road itself being well-nigh bare), and just as my wife concluded her poetic quotation over we turned. Luckily fortune again favored us, for my deviating from the right path without sufficient cause would have prevented my recovering for any damage we might have suffered.[1] One voluntarily encountering perils in the dark does so at his own risk.[2]

My wife impatiently suggested that she had better take the reins. I told her that she could reign at home, but that if she was driving and we really met with an accident, twelve jurymen would have to inquire into her capacity and the horses' character,[3] in considering whether ordinary care had been exercised, and the less said on the first subject the better.

"For goodness' sake, then, tell me what I can get if I am hurt on these abominable roads," she pettishly asked.

[1] Rice *v.* Montpelier, 19 Vt. 470; Tisdale *v.* Norton, 8 Met. 388.
[2] Mt. Vernon *v.* Dusouchett, 2 Cart. 586.
[3] Cobb *v.* Standish, 14 Me. 198.

"Well," I said, clearing my throat for a speech, "if the town is to blame for the state of the road, it is liable for the direct and immediate losses occasioned by the accident.[1] In some cases *I* could recover for the loss of your services and the expenses of your sickness;[2] although in Maine and Connecticut it has been decided otherwise.[3] If I myself were injured, I could get recouped for my loss of time and medical expenses.[4] Where the exertions of the plaintiff in endeavoring to rescue his horses, which had broken through a bridge, his exposure to the elements and his agitation — all the direct result of the defect in the bridge — produced epilepsy and made the man a wreck in body and mind (the doctors said the disease usually terminated in paralysis and mental imbecility), the jury gave the man $500 in compensation, and the judges thought it was none too much."[5]

"I should think not. It must be a poor body and mind to be worth no more than that."

"Where," I continued, "Mrs. Toms and her eight-year old boy were crossing a bridge in their buggy, the horse shied at some new planks on the bridge, backed to the edge and the hind wheels over a bank, Mrs. Toms tumbled out into the water some fourteen feet below, the jury

[1] Jenks *v.* Wilbraham, 11 Gray, 142.
[2] Hunt *v.* Winfield, 36 Wis. 154; Woodman *v.* Nottingham, 49 N. H. 387.
[3] Reed *v.* Belfast, 20 Me. 246; Chidsey *v.* Canton, 17 Conn. 475.
[4] Sandford *v.* Augusta, 32 Me. 536.
[5] Jaquish *v.* Ithaca, 36 Wis. 111.

considered that she had been driving in a proper manner and that the road ought to have had guards along the embankment. The court agreed with them, and held the township liable to make good her wounds and bruises; the want of railings was deemed the proximate cause of the injury, and not the horse becoming frightened or unmanageable.[1] A road which passes over a bank or bridge, or along a precipice, should always be properly guarded.[2] It seems that in the States of Vermont and Massachusetts corporations will be held liable for injuries (caused by defective ways) which are primarily imputable to pure accident (that is to an unexpected occurrence or event for which no one is responsible), if the accident happened without the fault of the injured one, and is such that common prudence could not have foreseen or guarded against, and if without the defect it would not have occurred.[3] Where, for instance, a runaway was crowded against the plaintiff's nag, owing to an obstruction in the road, the town was held liable; for streets should be so made as to be reasonably safe when such accidents, as may reasonably be expected occasionally to happen in the best regulated places, do occur.[4] And so when a carriage ran away with the people in it by itself and over an

[1] Toms *v.* Whitby, 35 Q. B. (Ont.) 195; *S. C.*, In Appeal, 37 Q. B. 100.
[2] Bliss *v.* Deerfield, 13 Pick. 102; Davis *v.* Hill, 41 N. H. 329.
[3] Palmer *v.* Andover, 2 Cush. 601.
[4] Kelsey *v.* Glover, 15 Vt. 708; Swift *v.* Newbury, 36 Vt. 355.

embankment.[1] And all roads ought to be wide enough to allow of the ordinary shyings and frights of horses with safety, for shying is one of the natural habits of the animal,[2] and it must be in such repair that even skittish creatures may be driven without any risk of danger from its condition.[3] The road, however, need not afford a perfectly clear track to a runaway horse." [4]

"I wish that horse would stop switching his tail about," remarked my wife.

"A very sensible desire on your part; for it has been decided in Massachusetts that the liability of a town for accidents arising from defects in a highway is removed if the defect could have been avoided had not the horse by throwing its tail over the reins freed itself from the driver's control and so knocked the carriage against the obstacles complained of." [5]

"It is a pity that judges have not something better to do than consider the shakings of a horse's tail," said my wife, who seemed to be growing cross.

"'T is a pity that they decided as they did, for one can scarcely believe that the tossing of tails over the reins is one of those extremely unlikely and abnormal acts which are considered

[1] Palmer *v.* Andover, 2 Cush. 601.

[2] Houfe *v.* Fulton, 29 Wis. 296; Stone *v.* Hubbardston, 100 Mass. 49; Kelley *v.* Fond du Lac, 31 Wis. 180.

[3] Lower Macungie Tp. *v.* Merkhoffer, 71 Penn. St. 277.

[4] Wharton on Neg. § 105.

[5] Fogg *v.* Nahant, 98 Mass. 578; *S. P.*, 106 Mass. 278.

acts of God, and which ordinary sagacity cannot foresee; it seems rather an ordinary incident of travel and so a contingency against which the road-maker should provide.[1] However, to continue the subject on which I was dilating, although a traveller is bound to have his carriage and harness in good road-worthy condition, or else bear quietly the pains and penalties,[2] still he need not always see that his carriage is perfect, his team of the most manageable character and in the best training, ere he goes out for a turn. If he uses ordinary care and prudence and an evil befalls him from the state of the road (coupled with some accidental cause), he can recover for his damages.[3] In Maine, however, the judges seem inclined to take a different view and absolve the town from liability where the accident would not have happened but for something going wrong with the horse or carriage; they say that if they are satisfied that an accident happened from a defect in the road and a defect in the harness making it unsafe, — although the driver knew not of it and thought all was right, — the injured one cannot sustain an action against the town.[4] Where one Moulton" —

"Do you mean Beecher's quondam friend?" asked my wife.

1 Wharton, § 106.
2 Welsh *v.* Lawrence, 2 Chitty, 262; Smith *v.* Smith, 2 Pick. 621.
3 Hunt *v.* Pownal, 9 Vt. 411.
4 Moore *v.* Abbot, 32 Me. 46.

"Oh, no; it was before the days of Mrs. Tilton's notoriety. This Moulton was driving on a bridge, and his horse, seeing another plunge into the water, became unmanageable and threw the wagon into the stream, there being no railing; the town had not to pay the damages.[1] And where a sleigh-bolt broke, and then the horse bolted and injured itself against a heap of stones in the road, the judges considered that the driver had not exercised due care, and therefore would have to settle the farrier's little bill himself.[2] Similarly, where a horse being instigated thereto by some evil spirit, refused to hearken to the reins and so went over an unprotected bank, whereon, perchance, the wild thyme grew, the poor owner of the nag was requested to show that the accident would equally have occurred if the horse had not been so uncontrollable, before he could get anything out of the town." [3]

A gentle snore from the partner of my joys and sorrows told me that I was wasting my eloquence and learning on the midnight air, so I forbore, and shortly after we reached our home safe and sound.

1 Moulton *v.* Sanford, 51 Me. 127; Horton *v.* Taunton, 97 Mass. 266, n.

2 Davis *v.* Dudley, 4 Allen, 557.

3 Titus *v.* Northbridge, 97 Mass. 258.

CHAPTER III.

INSURANCE.

What's an Accident? — Major Vis. — Exposure and Death. — Wholly disabled. — What can be recovered. — Heavy Weights. — Stumbling. — Pitchforked. — Change of Business. — Lost beneath the Dancing Waves. — A Man not a Private Conveyance. — Carelessness.

SHORTLY after the events related in my last chapter, I expected business to call me away from home. Accidents by rail — explosions, collisions, over-turnings, exploits of the fire-fiend — had become so much the reverse of angel's visits, that though some said I had the hanging mark upon me, I determined to make assurance doubly sure and take a bond of fate in the shape of an "accident ticket;" not that hope told a flattering tale, or that vain expectations of making anything by the transaction filled my soul, but as a preventive rather than a cure, for accidents seldom happen when one is prepared, as showers seldom descend when one is armed *cap-a-pie* with umbrella and thick boots.

Ere spending my twenty cents, however, I determined to find out what an accident, within the meaning of the ticket, really might be; but I discovered that no satisfactory definition of the word had ever been given by the courts. Cockburn, C. J., says that it means some violence, casualty, or *vis major;* and that disease or death, generated by exposure to heat, cold, damp, the vicissitudes of climate or atmospheric influences, cannot be called accidental, unless, perhaps, where the exposure is actually brought about by circumstances which might give it the character of accident, — as a shipwrecked mariner dying from exposure to cold and wet in a small boat upon the roaring, raging ocean.[1] This decision settled that I could recover nothing if my nose or my toes were frozen off; nor if my early demise was brought about by croup, measles, or small-pox, caught in the cars, could my family recover any remuneration for the loss of the house-band. If, like the good Samaritan's friend, I should chance to fall among thieves, who should strip me of my raiment, wound me, and depart leaving me dead, that, probably, would be considered a death by violent and accidental means, for Judge Withey, of Michigan, has laid it down that an accident is any event which takes place without the foresight or expectation of the person acted upon or affected by the event.[2] In Maryland it has been defined as an unusual and unexpected result attending the performance of a usual and necessary act; and there it has been decided that every injury caused by accident, save

[1] Sinclair *v.* Maritime Pass. Ass. Co., 3 El. & E. 478.

[2] Ripley *v.* Rw. Pass. Ass. Co., 2 Bigelow, Ins. Cases, 738.

those specially excepted by the policy, are covered by it.[1] And in New York an accident is said to be something which takes place without any intelligent or apparent cause, without design and out of course.[2]

I was pleased to find that I might recover for a "railway accident," if anything happened to me while travelling by the cars, although nothing happened to the train, for instance, if while getting out, after the cars had stopped, I should slip, fall, and injure myself, not through any negligence of my own, but because the steps were slippery;[3] and that any money to which I might become entitled under the policy would not in any way lessen the damages which I might claim against the carrier for any injuries received to my corpus.[4] This is only fair, as one pays premiums to insure himself on the understanding that his right to be compensated when he is injured is an equivalent for the premium paid. It is a *quid pro quo;* larger if he gets it, on the chance that he may never get it at all.[5] Where compensation to the insured is granted "in case of bodily injury of so serious a nature as wholly to disable the assured from following his usual business, occupation, or pursuits," I would be entitled to pay if so disabled that I could not

1 Prov. Life Ins. & Inv. Co. *v.* Martin, 32 Maryland, 310.
2 Mallory *v.* Travellers Ins. Co., 47 N. Y. 52.
3 Theobald *v.* Rw. Pass. Ass. Co., 10 Ex. 45.
4 Bradburn *v.* Gt. W. R., L. R., 10 Ex. 3, 11 Eng. Rep. 330.
5 Dalby *v.* Indian & L. Life Ass. Co., 15 C. B. 365.

get to my office to work, although I were well enough to transact business in my own bedroom, or clad in a *robe de nuit* instead of a professional toga.[1] For total disability from the prosecution of one's usual employment means inability to follow one's usual occupation, business, or pursuits in the usual way :[2] *i. e.*, *e. g.*, a farmer who can do nothing but milk, and a merchant who can only keep his books, are totally disabled within the meaning of such a provision as the above.[3] To be *wholly* or *quite disabled* is to be unable to do what one is called upon to do in the ordinary course of business, and this is by no means the same thing as being " unable to do any part of one's business." [4]

The decided cases made it clear that I could recover only for the personal expense and pain occasioned by the accident, and not damage for loss of time or of profit occasioned thereby ; and also, that if I insured my life for only $1000, it could not be assumed that my life was worth only that and nothing more, and an injury sustained estimated at a proportionate sum.[5]

I also, as a result of my researches, learned the following: If a policy provided that the company would be responsible for accidents operating from external causes, I would get something if I injured

[1] Hooper *v.* Accidental Death Ass. Co., 5 H. & N. 546; affirmed on appeal, 5 H. & N. 557.

[2] May on Insurance, p. 644.

[3] Sawyer *v.* United States Casualty Co., 8 Law Reg. (N. S.), 233.

[4] Per Wilde, B., Hooper *v.* Accidental Death Ins. Co., 5 H. & N. 546.

[5] Theobald *v.* Rw. Travellers Ins. Co., 10 Ex. 45.

my spinal marrow by lifting my trunk;[1] but it would appear that rupture caused by jumping from the cars while in motion and afterwards running to accomplish certain business, done voluntarily and in the ordinary way, and without any necessity therefor, and with no unforeseen or involuntary movement of the body, such as stumbling, or slipping, or falling, is not caused by violent or accidental means. Though it might be otherwise if in jumping I should lose my balance and fall, or strike some unseen object, or in running should stumble or slip.[2] If, while on my travels, I should take to amateur farming (not the most likely thing in the world, bucolic desires not filling my soul, and the thermometer being down below nothing), and while pitching hay let the handle of the pitchfork slip and pitch into my bowels, producing thereby peritoneal inflammation, whereof I should die, that would be an accidental death![3] Nor would the casual change of occupation from the pursuits of the forum to that of the field, forfeit my right to recover.[4] Where an accident produced hernia, which caused death, it was held that the death was not within the exception of the policy which provided that the company did not insure against death or disability

[1] Martin *v.* Travellers Ins. Co., 1 F. & F. 505.
[2] Southard *v.* Rw. Pass. Ass. Co., 34 Conn. 574.
[3] N. Am. L. & A. Ins. Co. *v.* Burroughs, 69 Penn. St. 43.
[4] Admins. of Stone *v.* U. S. Casualty Co., 34 N. J. 371; N. Am. L. & A. Ins. Co. *v.* Burroughs, *supra;* Provident Life Ins. Co. *v.* Fennel, 49 Ill. 180; Prov. Life Ins. & Inv. Co. *v.* Martin, 32 Md. 310.

arising from rheumatism, gout, hernia, etc.[1] If I should go in bathing and die from the action of the water causing asphyxia, that, too, would be a death by external violence within the meaning of the policy, whether I swam out too far, struck my head against a rock in diving, or — unskilled in the natatorial art — got out of my depth; but if I succumbed to an attack of apoplexy while taking the bath, that would not be a death from accident.[2] A provision that no claim is to be made under a policy, except in respect of an injury caused by some "outward and visible means," applies only to non-fatal injuries.[3]

I found also, that it was legally correct — however paradoxical it may appear — to say that I was travelling in a carriage, when in fact I was actually alighting therefrom;[4] and that I would be "travelling in a carriage provided for the transportation of passengers," if, while in the prosecution of my journey, I walked on foot, as passengers are wont to do from one station to another. The courts, ever ready to interpret a policy in the way most advantageous to the insured,[5] will not allow "travelling in a public conveyance" to be construed literally, and if an accident happens while one is

[1] Fitton *v* Acc. Death Ins. Co., 17 C. B. (N. S.), 122; but see Smith *v.* Acc. Ins. Co., L. R., 5 Ex. 302, a case of erysipelas.

[2] Trew *v.* Railway Pass. Ass. Co., 5 H. & N. 211, affirmed on appeal, 6 H. & N. 839.

[3] Mallory *v.* Traveller's Ins. Co., Ct. of Appeals, 47 N. Y. 52.

[4] Theobald *v.* Rw. Pass. Ass. Co., 10 Ex. 44.

[5] Hooper *v.* Accid. Death Ins. Co., 5 H. & N. 545; 6 Ib. 839; Smith *v.* Acc. Ins. Co., per Kelly, C. B., *supra.*

getting off or on a train, or attempting to do so for any reasonable purpose, it comes within the terms of a policy insuring against accidents while travelling by public conveyance.[1] Mr. John Wilder May (who has written a large book on Insurance) thinks that, perhaps, in a reasonable and substantially accurate sense a man may be said to be travelling by public conveyance, when he is prosecuting a journey by rail or boat, whether he is sitting still in a motionless car, or standing serenely on the station-platform, or walking to and fro thereon waiting for a start, or going into a station for prog, or returning therefrom after having grubbed;[2] although Chase, C. J., held that a man who had performed the greater part of a journey by steamboat and, there being no public conveyance, proceeded on foot to his house some miles distant from the port, could not exactly be said to be a private conveyance to himself while walking.[3] An elephant may be a traveller.[4]

A poor fellow away down in Kentucky inadvertently and needlessly put his arm out of a car window and had it injured by being bumped against a post, and the court held the injury not accidental, being attributable to the person's own negligence.[5] But as this case stands alone, it will

[1] Tooley *v.* Rw. Pass. Acc. Ins. Co., 2 Ins. L. J. 275.
[2] May on Insurance, p. 661
[3] Ripley *v.* Ins. Co., 16 Wall. (U. S.), 336.
[4] Gregory *v.* Adams, 14 Gray, 242.
[5] Morel *v* Mississippi Valley Life Ins. Co., 4 Bush (Ky.), 535.

scarcely answer to point a *moral* or adorn a tale, and the better opinion seems to be that contributory negligence is no defence, as the liability rests upon contract, one of the chief objects of which is to protect a man against his own carelessness or negligence.[1] But one must not be guilty of willful and wanton exposure of himself to unnecessary danger; for instance he must not ride on the engine, [2] or attempt to cross the track when an ap-approaching train is within fifty feet.[3]

I was now assured that to be insured was sure to bring contentment, if not riches.

1 Prov. Life Ins. & Inv. Co. *v.* Martin, 32 Md. 310; Trew *v.* Rw. Pass. Ass. Co., 6 H. & N. 839; Schneider *v.* Provident Life Ins. Co., 24 Wis. 28; Champlin *v.* Rw. Pass. Ass. Co., 6 Lansing (N. Y.), 71.

2 Brown *v.* Rw. Pass Ass. Co., 45 Mo. 221; May, p. 657.

3 May on Insurance, p. 667.

CHAPTER IV.

EVERYTHING MUST BE SOUND, AND EVERY ONE CAREFUL.

The Reason why. — Literature of Stages. — Off on Wheels. — Soundness warranted. — Seats taken. — Fare paid, either First or Last. — Damage to Trunks. — Involuntary Aeronautics. — Passengers injured. — Negligence of Passengers, or of Drivers. — Carriers liable for Smallest Fault; Not Insurers. — Genuine Accidents. — Horses left standing. — Driving and upsetting a Friend. — Non-repair of Roads. — Care required. — Tennysonian Stanzas. — Pleasures of the Weed and Rural Life.

THE long vacation was rapidly approaching, — that season when the heat having lengthened out the days (as it does everything else), the members of the legal profession abandon rejoinders and demurrers, cast briefs and records, with physic, to the dogs, and, satisfied with bills and conveyances, wander off in search of change in cooling streams and pastures green. In my modest household was eagerly discussed the question, "Whither shall we flee?"

My wife's step-mother's brother's wife's mother's aunt, had recently met with a horrible and excruciating death upon a railway car, so my wife had solemnly vowed never again to commit herself to the safe-keeping of a railway company; this, therefore, shut us off from the usual means of exit from our inland city, and yet as "*Exeunt omnes*," was the cry, we could not surely stay at home; if we did, we would have to lie low in the kitchen and back premises, that we might appear to others to be away. At last I found that there was still a tumble-down old stage-coach making, with the assistance of two skeleton horses, tri-weekly trips to and from the little Village of Ayr, where we could catch a steamboat and thus do in proper style the Lakes and the St. Lawrence, the Ottawa and the far-famed Saguenay.

When this discovery of mine was divulged at home, great was the rejoicing, loud pæans rose, and for days I was deluged with quotations from all the novelists, from old Fielding to poor Dickens anent stages, and coaches, and stage-coaches. I was told of all the heroes of romance, from Tom Brown back to Tom Jones, who had journeyed thereby; I was confidently informed, on the authority of Mr. William Makepeace Thackeray, that in every coach there is sure to be found an asthmatic old gentleman, a fat man, swelling preternaturally with great coats and snoring indecently, and a lone widow who insists upon all the windows being shut, and fills the vehicle with the fumes of rum which she sucks perpetually from a black bottle. Mr. Thomas Hughes was quoted to prove how much more punctual stages are than railway trains, for he tells of one that went "ten miles an hour, including stoppages, and so punctual that all the road set their watches by her." The old joke concerning the young man who, on being asked if he had ever been through Euclid, replied, "Yes, I have driven through it on a stage-coach," was given to me once again as if uttered for the first time; and I was informed that an Indian squaw, the first time she saw a coach pass at a spanking trot, and watched the wheels revolving rapidly, clapped her hands in delight, exclaiming, "Run, little one, run! or the big one will catch you!" The subject gradually became monotonous.

At length, however, the day of our departure dawned.

When the coach drove up to the door, at sight of the dusty tumble-down conveyance, my wife — true to her woman's nature — was half inclined to decline to trust her precious self therein, but as I had paid our fares when booking our places — the driver having asked for the money, as he had a perfect right to do [1] — and as I assured her every stage-coach proprietor warrants that his stage is sufficiently secure to perform the journey proposed, and is bound to examine his vehicles every day, and if he does not is responsible for accidents,[2] she consented to start; although I could see from her expression of countenance that

[1] Chitty on Contracts, 292.

[2] Bremner *v.* Williams, 1 C. & P. 414; Sharp *v.* Grey, 9 Bing. 457.

the ideal coach which she had been fondly cherishing was very different to the one into which we entered. Our luggage was mounted on top, and soon we were rumbling down the street to pick up other passengers, as we were numbers one and two. A sudden stop to mend some broken harness called forth an exclamation of disgust from the fair being beside me, and a remark from myself to the effect that she need not be anxious, as the owner was responsible that all the equipments of the conveyance, drivers, horses, harness, were fit and suitable.[1]

In a few minutes we drew up at the door of a large mansion from which quickly emerged four old maids; they drew back in horror when they saw my pantaloons, one exclaiming: —

"Driver, we engaged the whole inside of the coach, and there 's a man in it."

"Yes, mum," said John, "but one of you can sit outside along of me for a bit; the gentleman is not going far."

"You have no right to separate us[2] or let other persons get inside," replied number one, waxing wrathy.

"No, indeed," chorused the others.

"Ladies," I said, "I will be most happy to give up my place and ride outside; the driver should have told me that the inside had been en-

[1] Crofts *v.* Waterhouse, 3 Bing. 321; Jones *v.* Boyce, 1 Stark. 493; Stokes *v.* Saltonstall, 13 Peters, 181; Ingalls *v.* Bills, 9 Met. 1.

[2] Long *v.* Horne, 1 C. & P. 611.

gaged, and then my wife and myself would have waited until some other day."

"Well," quoth the driver, "the ladies had not paid for the seats, and we were not bound to keep them for them."[1]

With withering sarcasm the eldest maid replied, "Here is your money, sir."

If a look could have annihilated a coachee, never again would that man have mounted a box, or handled the ribbons, after the Medusa glance he then received. I emerged from the inside, into which the ladies stowed themselves and several parcels, packages and bandboxes, while several boxes of larger growth, containing their staple goods, were hoisted up aloft. After picking up a man we rattled off down the street into the open country.

The last comer had not as yet paid his fare, and at the first stopping-place he was asked for it; but he demurred, saying that as he had not prepaid the fare, it was not due until the whole journey was completed.

"You will have to leave the stage then," said the collector.

"I 'll do nothing of the kind," returned the other, "and if you force me off it will be at your peril, for your driver permitting me to commence the journey without prepayment is an acquiescence in my riding to the end before paying up,

[1] Ker v. Mountain, 1 Esp. 27.

so you may *howl and* swear as much as you like."[1]

At this the man of fares subsided, and we resumed our slow jog-trot without any diminution of numbers. The jolting of our vehicle soon caused one of the trunks belonging to one or other of the four sisters to gape and yawn in a manner which exposed the contents thereof in a way which would doubtless have caused the fair owner to blush to the roots of her hair (if it was her own she wore), and it appearing probable that articles of feminine apparel would soon be scattering themselves over the dusty road, and knowing that the box not having been securely and properly packed and fastened, the carrier would not be liable for any loss or damage happening to it,[2] I persuaded the driver to stop until the mischief could be remedied; for such an injury would vex a saint, much more a shrew of her impatient humor. With much grumbling he consented, and all was soon made taut and right.

To make up for lost time, we now rushed ahead at a terrific pace, considering the clumsy, cumbrous, jingling, jerking concern in which we were travelling. The ladies within (who were crushing their bonnets, elbowing each other under the fifth rib, jumping up and bouncing into one another's

[1] Howland *v.* Brig Lavinia, 1 Peters Adm. 126; Detouches *v.* Peck, 9 Johnson, 210.

[2] Walker *v.* Jackson, 10 M. & W. 161.

laps with every plunge of the coach), cried one and all: —

"Oh, do be careful — don't go so fast." And I, in admonitory tones, told the driver that we would hold him liable for any injuries that might happen to either ourselves or our baggage, in consequence of his racing in such an improper manner.[1]

"All right," said he, "I'm responsible, and I am master too, here; so I'll do just what I like."

Scarce had he uttered these words when we drew near a large spreading tree, standing in the middle of the road. At a glance I saw that the coach must pass under the outstretched branches, and that they were so low that they would assuredly sweep the top of the stage clear of luggage and whatsoever else was thereupon, and unfortunately I myself was thereupon. I had no choice left but to jump off or remain in certain peril; mindful of my early performances in the gymnasium, of the two threatening evils I chose what appeared the lesser, and as the foremost twigs took off the hat of the driver (who was considerably below where I was perched), I sprang to the ground, and, as if in rage at my escape, the giant forest tree hurled two or three trunks after me; one came with a thud upon my foot and bruised it rather badly.

Of course the ladies screamed loudly as they

[1] Mayor *v.* Humphries, 1 C. & P. 251; Gough *v.* Bryan, 5 Dowl. 765.

saw me flying in a graceful parabolic curve through the azure air. The driver as rapidly as possible pulled up his old horses. Some loud conversation took place between myself and the man, interspersed with ejaculations more vigorous than religious, he contending that I had only myself to thank for my injuries, as if I had bent low enough I would not have been touched by the tree.

"All very well," I replied, "if I had been the size of the little husband no bigger than a thumb what was put into a quart pot and made to beat a drum, but Mr. Thomas Thumb himself, if he had been on top, could not have escaped from that tree. However, your master is liable to me for the injuries I have received."[1]

"No, he is n't," surlily replied the Jehu, "because I say if you had staid quiet you would not have been hurt."

"Even if that were so, it would make no difference, as I entertained a well-founded apprehension of being decapitated by that ugly branch."[2]

I argued not, however, with the man, but limping back to the coach, remounted to my elevated seat, accompanied by the prayers and entreaties of my wife, not to blight her young life by exposing myself to any more such frightful risks outside, but to come within where she was sure there

[1] Ingalls *v.* Bills, 9 Met. 1; Stokes *v.* Saltonstall, 13 Pet. (U. S.) 181; Frink *v.* Potter, 17 Ill. 406.

[2] Jones *v.* Boyce, 1 Stark. 493.

was plenty of room; but I preferred the fresh air and fine view aloft to the close musty smell and narrow field of vision down below.

When again under way, my fellow-passenger, who by sitting on the box with the driver had avoided the collision, began to tell me of his grandmother, one Mistress Elizabeth Dudley, who on one occasion was an outside passenger to the Cross Keys, Chelsea. When in front of the gateway leading to the stable-yard of that inn, the coachman requested the travellers to alight, as the passage into the yard was awkward. As Mrs. Dudley did not wish to soil her pumps in the dirty road, she said she would rather be driven into the yard. Coachee told her to stoop, and then lashed up his horses. The coach was 8 feet 9 in. high, and the archway only 9 feet 9 in., and Betsy, not being able to squeeze herself into the interstice of twelve inches, received a severe injury by having her back and shoulders knocked against the archway; she recovered, however, with £100 damages.[1]

I said: "Of course, to excuse the driver from responsibility, it must always be shown that the plaintiff was guilty of negligence which contributed directly to the injury.[2] I remember one case where a man was asked by the driver to ride inside a coach, and told that if he remained out-

[1] Dudley *v.* Smith, 1 Camp. 167.

[2] Colegrove *v.* N. Y. & Harlem, etc., R. R. Co., 6 Duer, 382.

side it would be at his own risk; he treated both the request and the hint with silent contempt, and being injured by the overturning of the carriage, sued the owners and got damages, as it appeared that the accident occurred from the negligence of the driver, and that the position of the obstreperous man in no way contributed to it."[1]

"It is clearly settled," returned my new made acquaintance, "that a driver, or his master, although he does not warrant the absolute safety of his passengers is, nevertheless, answerable for the smallest negligence;[2] and that the proprietor is also responsible for all defects in the coach, even though they be out of sight and not discoverable upon an ordinary examination, as a *sharp* fellow once proved."[3]

"An American, however, *in gall* and bitterness was told by a court, that carriers, although bound to use the utmost care and diligence to prevent those injuries which human care and foresight can guard against, still are not liable for injuries happening through hidden defects which could not from the most careful and thorough examination be discovered."[4]

"Yes," interrupted my friend, "but in the State of Illinois, a *Potter*, who owned a stage-

[1] Keith *v.* Pinkham, 43 Maine, 501; Lackawana & B. R. R. Co. *v.* Chenewirth, 52 Penn. St. 382.

[2] Harris *v.* Costar, 1 C. & P. 636; Christie *v.* Griggs, 2 Camp. 79.

[3] Sharp *v.* Grey, 9 Bing. 457.

[4] Ingalls *v.* Bills, 9 Met. 1.

coach, was held liable for an injury to a passenger, which resulted from the breaking of an axle-tree, through the effect of frost."[1]

"Long ago the courts in England held that a man established a *primâ facie* case by proving his taking passage in a coach, his coming to grief while in it, and the injury he sustained; and then that the proprietor must show, if he could, that his vehicle was as good as a vehicle could be, and that the driver was as skillful a handler of the reins as could be found."[2]

"Yes, as Best, C. J., once said, a coachman must have competent skill and must use that skill with discretion; he must be well acquainted with the road he undertakes to drive; he must be provided with steady horses, a coach and harness of sufficient strength and properly made, and also with lights by night. If there be the least failure in any one of these things, the duty of the proprietor is not fulfilled, and he is answerable for any injury or damage that happens.[3] He also is so unless the driver exercised a sound discretion at the time of the accident. If he could have exercised a sounder judgment or better discretion than he did, as by driving slower or faster, or by telling his passengers to dismount at a dangerous or difficult place, the owner must make compensation."[4]

[1] Frink *v.* Potter, 17 Ill. 406.
[2] Christie *v.* Griggs, 2 Camp. 79.
[3] Crofts *v.* Waterhouse, 3 Bing. 319; Farish *v.* Reigle, 11 Gratt. 697.
[4] Stanton *v.* Weller, Hil. Term, 6 Vict. U. C.

"Fortunately, however, for the pockets of carriers, they are not considered as actual insurers of the safety of those who intrust their precious bodies to them. Accidents will happen in the best regulated concerns, and it appears to be settled that when they do occur where there is *no* negligence or default, the law will protect carriers from the demands of injured ones." [1]

"Oh, yes, that is a well-established doctrine, and many cases might be quoted to sustain it. Where, for instance, on a dark night the lights were obscured by a fog, or the coachman without any fault of his gets off the road." [2]

"And also," I chimed in, "where extreme cold prevented the driver doing his duty; [3] and where the reflection of the sun upon falling water frightened the horses so that they ran away and knocked things into pie; [4] and where an axle-tree that was sound and perfect snapped asunder.[5] And where a sleigh or a carriage upsets through mere accident and without culpable neglect on the part of the driver — as where he had been driving along a track in a ditch to take advantage of the small modicum of snow remaining and in turning on to the road again got into a hidden hole and upset — and the horses escape from the hands of the Jehu,

1 Aston *v.* Heaven, 2 Esp. 533.
2 Crofts *v.* Waterhouse, 3 Bing. 321.
3 Stokes *v.* Saltonstall, 13 Peters, 181.
4 Aston *v.* Heaven, *supra.*
5 Parker *v.* Flagg, 26 Me. 181; Add. on Contracts, 495.

and run away and do mischief to the person or property of other people; though undoubtedly the owner would be liable where there was clear negligence on the part of himself or driver which led to the carriage being overturned and the escape of his horses.[1] If a man has carelessly left his horses standing on the highway, while he is drinking or loafing in a tavern, and the horses run away and commit an injury, the right to recover damages is clear.[2] Even if a third party causes the stampede of the horses which are left standing alone, the owner will be liable for all damage done;[3] and it will be inferred that a horse was negligently fastened if it gets loose and runs away.[4] But where a pony and chaise were left standing in the street without any person to take care of them, and afterwards the pony was seen running away with the chaise, and those who saw the runaway did not know the cause of the starting. The owner of the turnout, however, proved that his wife was holding the nag by the bridle, when a Punch and Judy show coming up frightened the pony, which breaking from the lady ran off, and Lord Denman in charging the jury, said: 'If the facts are true as suggested by the defense, I very much think you will be disposed to consider this an inevitable accident; one which the defendants could not prevent.'"[5]

1 Robinson *v.* Bletcher, 15 U. C. Q. B. Rep. 160.

2 Ibid.

3 Illidge *v.* Goodwin, 5 C. & P. 190; Park *v.* O'Brien, 23 Conn. 339.

4 Strup *v.* Edens, 22 Wis. 432.

5 Goodman *v.* Taylor, 5 C. & P. 410; Kennedy *v.* Way, Brightley (Pa.), 186.

"Of course if one gentleman when out driving offers another a seat in his carriage, he is not liable at all for an accident afterwards occurring; unless, indeed, it were of a gross description; and, as nothing is more usual than for accidents to happen in driving, without any want of care on the part of the driver, no *primâ facie* presumption of negligence is raised when an accident does occur, so the injured one must give affirmative evidence of gross negligence on the part of his obliging friend."

"Oh, yes; that is well settled by a case where the Privy Council reversed the decision of the Supreme Court of Victoria. A gentleman was conveying the plaintiff, who was a decorator and gardener in his employ, to perform for him certain work. The defendant, the gentleman, drove, and while on the road the king-bolt broke, the horses bolted, the carriage was overturned, the plaintiff thrown out and stunned; and when the man came to himself the horses and forewheels of the buggy had vanished. There being no evidence of gross negligence, the decorator had to bear his injuries and bruises unavenged.[1] One cannot fairly be expected to examine very strictly and carefully the state of the bolts and fastenings of his carriage every time he goes out with it."[2]

"By the way," said my companion, "your own right to recover is perfectly clear, for I am sure

[1] Moffatt *v.* Bateman, L. R., 3 P. C. App. 115. [2] Ibid.

that I have seen in some place or other that where a woman was jolted off a stage and had her leg fractured by some luggage that was thrown on it, she was successful in a suit against the owners of the vehicle."[1]

"Thanks for the information," I replied, "I did not know that there was a case so exactly on all fours with my own."

"A little research nowadays will enable one to find a decision on almost every possible point the mind of man can conceive, so great is the number of the reports now accumulating with fearful rapidity upon the shelves of law libraries. Ah me! the speed with which the yearly accretions of reports fill up every library, not of Brobdignagian proportions, is an appalling phenomenon. It makes me sigh to consider the lot of our grandchildren who may chance to commence the study of law! I"—

A sudden jerk and bump, caused by a wheel hitting against a stump in the middle of the road, stopped the sentence and set us talking about the liability of road companies and municipalities as to keeping the roads in a proper, safe, and convenient condition.

"Yes," said my friend, "towns are not absolved from their responsibility because some one else is bound by law to keep the road smooth and safe.[2] But of course the liability is limited to in-

[1] Curtis *v.* Drinkwater, 2 B. & Ad. 169.

[2] Wallace *v.* New York, 2 Hilton, 440; Phillips *v.* Veazie, 40 Me. 96.

juries caused by defects and obstructions for which the town might be indicted, or which by law they are bound to remove."[1]

"I remember," I said, "hearing of a man who lost his horse in a deep mud-hole filled with water and partly in the highway, which he took for a watering-place, recovering its value from the city."[2]

"Yes; if it had been a hired nag, for the value of which the driver had to pay the owner, his rights and his wrongs would have been just the same.[3] If this coach had been upset just now, the road company would have been liable to the coach proprietor for all injuries to this venerable structure on which we are perched, but not for any damages which we might recover against him for bruises and scratches, dislocations and broken bones that might fall to our lot."[4]

"Still there are some cases of accidental damage which the law regards as mere misfortunes, or pure accidents, where no negligence or fault is imputable to any one; as where a man was thrown out of his wagon and broke his collar-bone in consequence of the wheel getting into a small rut. The court will not assume that the badness of the road is proved beyond a peradventure merely because an accident took place while the driver was exercising due care."[5]

1 Merrill *v.* Hampden, 26 Me. 236; Davis *v.* Bangor, 42 Me. 522.
2 Cobb *v.* Standish, 14 Me. 198.
3 Littlefield *v.* Biddeford, 29 Me. 310.
4 Talmadge *v.* Zanesville & M. Road Co., 11 Ohio, 197.
5 Chappel *v.* Oregon, 36 Wis. 145.

"One is not required, however, to exercise extraordinary care and prudence.[1] And as old Lord Ellenborough says, before one can recover damages he must not only show that there was an obstruction that caused the trouble, but also that he himself was not lacking in ordinary care and in endeavoring to avoid it."[2]

"I always think highly of Ellenborough's decisions," I said, "although he was such a ninny that when in 'the Devil's Invincibles' (a famous volunteer corps), he was ever in the awkward squad; and Eldon used to say that he thought Ellenborough more awkward than himself, but others thought it was difficult to determine which of the two was entitled to bear the palm."

"Ah, yes! 'the Devil's Invincibles' was the corps in which there were some attorneys, and when Lieutenant-colonel Cox, Master in Chancery, who commanded, gave the word 'Charge,' two-thirds of the rank and file took out their note-books and wrote '6*s.* 8*d.*'"

"Ha! ha! that is as good as the story of the volunteer company of lawyers, who, when the drill-sergeant gave the command 'Right about face,' all stood still, and cried, 'Why?'"

"Unlike the six hundred,

> 'Theirs was to make reply,
> Theirs but to reason why,
> Theirs not to do, nor die.'"

[1] Cremer *v.* Portland, 36 Wis. 92.
[2] Butterfield *v.* Forrester, 11 East, 60

"You might add the concluding lines of that noble poem," I said.

> "'When can their glory fade?
> Oh the huge charge they made!
> All the world wondered.
> Pay them the charge they made!
> Pay them the bill they made!
> Noble attorneys'"

"Good. Very good. Do you smoke."

And he added to the effect of his question by handing me a well filled case of choice cheroots. Soon we were both lazily puffing at our cigars, and dreamily enjoying ourselves as we drove along past woodland and meadow, up hill and down, over sparkling, bubbling streamlets, beside fields of waving grain.

The day was charming. The heat of the July sun was tempered by a cooling breeze which blew softly upon us as we journeyed. The dust had been laid to rest by the sprinkling of an early shower; the birds carolled gayly amid their leafy bowers; here and there the squirrel peeped forth from his hiding-place and chattered at us as we passed, or raced ahead along the zig-zag fence; at one moment fluttered by a

> Butterfly ranging on his yellow wings.
> A primrose gone alive with joy, to dance with living things;

then came large white ones "which looked as if the May-flower had caught life, and palpitated forth upon the winds."

And my friend dreamily muttered, "Would

that I were an insect! Fancy the fun of tucking one's self up for a night in the leaves of a rose, and being rocked to sleep by the gentle sighs of summer air; and having nothing to do when you awake but to wash yourself in a dewdrop, and then eat your bedclothes."

Ever and anon we heard the truly rural sounds of the whetstone against the scythe, and the lowing of the kine, or the plaintive cry of some wandering lamb. All these arcadian sights and sounds acted as a gentle lullaby upon our senses already soothed by nicotine, and we slept.

CHAPTER V.

NEARLY DRIVEN TO DEATH, AND HOW TO PASS.

Narrow Escape. — Look out for the Locomotive when the Bell rings. — Railway not liable when Driver in Fault. — Horses frightened by Engine. — Ferry-boats and Men. — On the Wrong Side. — The Laws of the Road. — Fatal Indecision. — Lien on Trunks. — Reflections on Lawyers.

We had a sharp awakening from our calm repose. A shrill cry of "Stop!" a jerk that nearly threw us to the ground as the driver reined in his horses, the wild fierce screech of an engine, the rumbling roar of a train as it dashed by, recalled us effectually from our wanderings in dream-land to the fact that we had been near a sudden and a fearful death. The driver had been nodding sleepily on his box and had not noticed that we were so near a railway crossing, and so had not looked out for the train; and when aroused, the horses' feet were actually upon the track and the cars but some seventy yards distant. The train as it rushed past almost scraped the horses' noses, so little had he been able to back them. On looking round I saw that the track must have been visible for some time before we came upon it, and one of the ladies said that she had heard a whistle a few seconds previously.

Of course, as might be expected, we all launched forth against Master Coachee, who was too frightened to reply. I said: —

"Don't you know that you are bound to keep your eyes open? It is your duty, and a duty dictated by common sense and prudence, on approaching a crossing, to do so carefully and cautiously, both for the sake of your own passengers and those travelling by rail."[1]

"Yes," chimed in my friend, "Chief Baron Pollock says, that a railway track *per se* is a warning of danger to those about to go upon it, and cautions them to see whether a train is coming."[2]

"One must judge and act reasonably in crossing a track," I continued. "One must not blindly and willfully drive upon it whether there is danger to be apprehended from his doing so or not. If one willfully goes upon the line of rails, as you were about to do, when danger is imminent and obvious, and sustains damage, he must bear the consequences of his own rashness and folly.[3] In fact, of late it seems to have been held that a man crossing a railway where there are no gates or flag-

[1] Nicholls *v.* Gt. Western Rw., 27 U. C. Q. B. 393; Boggs *v.* Gt. Western Rw. Co., 23 U. C. C. P. 573; Ellis *v.* Gt. Western Rw. Co., L. R., 9 C. P. 551; Johnston *v.* Northern Rw. Co., 34 U C. Q. B. 432; Penn. Rw. Co. *v.* Beale, 9 Can. L. J. (N. S.), 298.

[2] Stubley *v.* London and Northwestern Rw., L. R. 1 Ex. 16; questioning Bilbee *v.* London, B., & S. C. Rw. Co., 18 C. B. (N. S.), 584.

[3] Winckler *v.* Gt. Western Rw., 18 U. C. C. P. 261; Dascomb *v.* Buffalo & State Line R. R. Co., 27 Barb 221; Mackey *v.* N. Y. & C. R R. Co., 27 Barb. 528.

men must stop, listen, and keep a sharp lookout for the trains." [1]

"And," quoth my new friend, "a traveller is not exonerated from the duty of looking up and down the rails before going upon them, by reason of the engineer omitting to ring the bell or blow the whistle; nor is the company in such a case liable for injuries,[2] unless it is shown that the engineer's omission had a tendency to produce the loss or damage." [3]

"The Court of Appeals in the State of New York, however, holds that a traveller on a public road has a right to rely upon railway companies obeying the law and giving the necessary warnings when a train is approaching a crossing.[4] And if through negligence horses are frightened at a crossing, the railway company is responsible for all damages arising.[5] Moreover, the late Sir J. B. Robinson, C. J., of Ontario thought that where the proper signals were neglected, the company could not excuse themselves by showing that the injured one did not manage so well as he might have done, or that his horse was restive or unsteady; [6] and" —

[1] Pittsburg, F. W., & C. Rw. v. Dunn, 56 Penn. St. 280; Balt. & Ohio R. R. v. Breinig, 25 Md. 378; Skelton v. L. & N. W. Rw., L. R., 2 C. P. 631; Johnston v. Northern Rw., 34 U. C. Q. B. 439; Penn. R. v. Ackerman, 74 Penn. St. 265.

[2] Havens v. Erie Rw., 41 N. Y. 296; Grippen v. N. Y. C., 40 N. Y. 34; Parker v. Adams, 12 Met. 415; Johnston v. Northern Rw., *supra;* Bellefontaine Rw. v. Hunter, 33 Ind. 335; Miller v. G. T. R., 25 C. P. (Ont.) 389.

[3] Galena & Ch. Rw. v. Loomis, 13 Ill. 548.

[4] Hart v. Erie Rw. Co., 3 Albany L. J. 312. See also Tabor v. Mo. Valley Rw., 46 Mo. 353; *S. C.*, 2 Am. Rep. 270.

[5] Sneesby v. Lancashire & Y., etc., 1 Q. B. Div. 42.

[6] Tyson v. G. T. Rw., 20 U. C. Q. B. 256. See also, Ernst v. Hudson River Rw., 35 N. Y. 9.

Here a low wailing cry of "Oh, we might have all been killed — been killed — been killed" — uttered by one of the old maids, the others joining in the chorus, struck upon our ears. I chimed in with: —

"And if we had, allow me to inform you ladies, that neither we ourselves nor those who come after us could recover damages against the company therefor, because it would have been owing to the gross carelessness of our driver,[1] and we would be considered as being in the same position as he is and partakers with him in his sins."[2]

"That 's so," said my friend. "Every traveller in a conveyance is so far identified with the man who drives or directs it, that if any injury is sustained by him from collision with another vehicle, through the joint negligence of the drivers of the two traps, so that his driver could not maintain an action against the other driver, the passenger is himself equally prevented suing."[3]

"What a shame!" chorused the Graces, plus one. "And is there nobody you can punish?" they querulously queried.

"Oh, yes; you can sue your own driver, or his employer. You have a clear and undoubted remedy against them."[4]

1 Winckler v. Gt. Western Rw., 18 U. C. C. P. 261; Nicholls v. Gt. Western Rw., 27 Q. B. U. C. 382.

2 Stubley v. London & N. W. Rw., L. R., 1 Ex. 13.

3 Thorogood v. Bryan, 8 C. B. 115, cited Id. 131; Rigby v. Hewitt, 5 Ex. 240; Greenland v. Chaplin, Ib. 247; Armstrong v Lancashire & Y. Rw., L. R., 10 Ex. 47.

4 Maule, J., in Thorogood v. Bryan, 8 C. B. 131.

"Much good it would do you to sue me," growled the man. "You can't take the breeks off a Heelander."

"It has always seemed to me," I remarked to the legal gentleman beside me, "to be highly unreasonable that by a legal fiction the passenger should be so identified with the driver. What do you think on that point?"

"I quite agree with you," he returned, "and with my celebrated namesake, Mr. Smith, and I think that the question why both the wrong-doers should not be considered liable to a person free from all blame — not answerable for the acts of either of them — and whom they have both injured, should be more seriously considered than it has yet been."[1]

"I was glad to see that recently in New Jersey where a man on a street car was injured by a railway train, the court held that the negligence of the car-driver could not prevent the man from getting damages, the driver not being his servant."[2]

"By the way," said my friend, "did you notice how near we came to the post of the railway crossing sign-board, as the man backed the horses from the track? I think such posts are a perfect nuisance."

"They are not necessarily an indictable nui-

[1] Note to Ashby *v.* White, 1 Smith's Leading Cases (6th ed.), 353.
[2] Bennett *v.* N. Y., etc., 36 N. J. 225.

sance; and as the law allows them to erect such a sign, they would not be liable for any accident arising from the posts obstructing part of the road, at least if they were placed in a reasonably proper manner with a due regard to all the surrounding circumstances.[1] How the steam came out of the engine! It is a wonder that the horses were not more frightened!" I added.

"Length of days, hard work, and shortness of commons have doubtless curbed their spirits. I remember on one occasion some railway employees were endeavoring to put an engine on the track near a crossing, when my friend Mrs. Stott and another lady drove up in a wagon; they asked if they might cross. One man said 'Yes,' and then laughingly winked at the others. Mrs. S. got out and led the horse, but before they had passed over steam was let off through the sides of the locomotive; the horse got frightened, jumped upon my friend, knocked her down, ran over her and away. The court held the railway liable for this injury; the company tried to avoid the verdict by saying that the damages arose from the unnecessary and wanton act of their servants; but the judges inclined to the opinion that even if the act had been unnecessary and wanton, reckless and improper, still as it was done in the course of the servants' employment, and for the purpose of promoting it, the company must bear

[1] Soule *v.* G. T. R., 21 C. P. (Ont.), 308.

all the responsibility.[1] Of course, however, companies are not liable for accidents caused by horses getting frightened at the smoke, steam, or noise of their trains, when their servants do nothing amiss." [2]

Presently we came to a broad river unspanned by any bridge; we had to cross, therefore, in an old-fashioned ferry. All dismounted. I noticed that the little wharf to which the scow was attached was much the worse for wear, but the nymphs and naiads fell in love with none of us, so no one broke through, fortunately for the ferryman, for he would have been liable for any accident.[3]

"Ha!" said my friend, as the stage gave a great bump in lighting on the boat. "My Christopher Columbus, you ought to have your flats so that all drivers and carriages may embark with ease; and that jolt rattled the ivories in Jehu's jaw." [4]

"Shut up yours, and shell out," was the laconic response.

"How deeply seated is habit," spake Mr. Smith. "The bee makes honey just as sweet now as when Samson stole it from the lion; and this pitiless navigator must be paid his fare before

[1] Stott *v.* G. T. R., 24 U. C. C. P. (Ont.), 347; Limpus *v.* London Omnibus Co., 1 H. & C. 526.

[2] Burton *v.* Phila., etc., R. R. Co., 4 Harring. (Del.), 252.

[3] Pate *v.* Henry, 5 Stew. & Port. 101.

[4] Miles *v.* James, 1 McCord, 157.

we start,[1] just as old Charon had to receive his obolus ere he would ferry his fleshless passengers across the gloomy Styx."

"You 're too fleshy to lean up agin those thair sticks, unless you want to take a header backwards," quoth the ferryman.

"Oh!" exclaimed Smith, starting inwards as the rail started outwards, "you ought — you should — you are bound by law to have your boat, and your slips, and your landing stages, and everything else, safe and secure, not only for passengers, but also for their horses and carriages, luggage and merchandise;[2] and you are liable for any damage happening to a vehicle, or the horses, as soon as they are on board, although the driver still keeps charge."[3]

The latter part of the remark seemed called forth by the coach having begun to slip backwards towards the water.

"That thair is open to argyment," said the boatman. "I guess I knows my bizness. Some old judges say that a ferryman is not liable unless the animals be put in his charge;[4] nor where the driver don't take care.[5] Nor yet where the critters are so spry that they keant be trusted on a boat,[6] which I calkerlate them thair nags aint."

1 Pain *v.* Patrick, 3 Mod. 289.
2 Willoughby *v.* Horridge, 12 C. B. 751; Addison on Torts, 493.
3 Cohen *v.* Hume, 1 McCord, 439; Fisher *v.* Clisbee, 12 Ill. 344.
4 White *v.* Winnisimmet Co., 7 Cush. 155.
5 Wilson *v.* Hamilton, 4 Ohio St. 722.
6 Fisher *v.* Clisbee, *supra.*

"Down in Mississippi, a ferryman had to pay for two stage-horses that jumped overboard, and the court said that as soon as the property is put on the boat, the boatman has it *primâ facie* in his charge, and is responsible for it, unless the owner consents to take exclusive charge." [1]

"I guess I wish we poor chaps could make a prime and fashious charge. I have to work this old machine mornin', noon, and night, barring when it is too windy, or I have gone to roost, as I live away over there." [2]

Safely we passed o'er the flood, and safely disembarked and reseated ourselves in the venerable trap, which with creaks and groans — as though rheumatic pains shot through every bolt and bar — ascended the bank.

Just then we passed a heavy wagon. It was on the wrong side of the road, and we narrowly escaped collision. I sung out to the farmer driving it: —

"If you want to drive on the wrong side, old fellow, you should take more care and keep a better lookout,[3] for if an accident had happened, as we had not ample room to avoid your wheels, you would have been liable for the injury, being on the wrong side of the road." [4]

"Fine day, sir," was the only response that

[1] Powell *v.* Mills, 37 Miss. 691.
[2] Pate *v.* Henry, 5 Stew. & P. 101.
[3] Pluckwell *v.* Wilson, 5 C. & P. 375.
[4] Chaplin *v.* Hawes, 3 C. & P. 554.

came, and our driver, with a grin, told me that the old man was as deaf as a door-nail.

My companion turned and said to me, "I have often wondered why the rules of the road should be so different in England from what they are in America. In the old country the three laws are: First, on meeting, each party shall bear to the left; second, in passing, the passer shall do so on the right hand; and, third, in crossing, the driver shall bear to the left and pass behind the other carriage.[1] In America, the first rule is the reverse, that is, each party must keep to the right;[2] but in passing, the foremost person bears to the left, and the other passes on the off side, and in crossing, the driver bears to the left hand and passes behind the other carriage — at least so says Story."[3]

"'T is singular that there should be the difference," I remarked.

"But that is not the only point of diversity. In England these rules apply as well to equestrians as to carriages; while in the United States a traveller on horseback when meeting another equestrian, or a carriage, may exercise his own notions of prudence, and turn to the right or to the left.[4] Of course common consent and imme-

[1] Wayde *v.* Carr, 2 Dowl. & Ry. 255.

[2] Kennard *v.* Benton, 25 Maine, 39; and in Ontario, by Con. St. U. C. ch. 56, in meeting, conveyances must turn to right, and so when one is overtaken by another.

[3] Story on Bail. § 599.

[4] Dudley *v.* Bolles, 24 Wend. 465.

morial usage require that a horseman should yield the road to a wagon or other vehicle.[1] If, however, he is mulish and will not turn out when he might safely do so, and his steed is injured by a collision, he is remediless.[2] Again, when one is ahead in America he need not, unless he has some milk of human nature in his veins, turn out at all to let a man behind pass, if there is room enough on either side."

"But if there is no room, what then?" I queried.

"Why, then, if it is practicable, the front one must give an equal portion of the road to his fellow biped behind; and if it is not practicable, number two must follow in Job's steps and exercise the Christian grace of patience, and wait until a more favorable spot is reached. If number one will not turn out when he can, he is answerable at law for it. His pursuer, however, must not take the matter into his own hands and attempt to force his way past." [3]

"It is," I said, "fortunate, however, that these laws of the road are not inflexible like those of the Medes and Persians of antique days, but may on occasions be departed from." [4]

"Yes; if there is no other carriage in the way, or if the road is broad enough, one may go on

[1] Washburn *v.* Tracy, 2 D. Chip. 128.

[2] Beach *v.* Parmeter, 23 Penn. St. 196; Grier *v.* Sampson, 27 Pa. 183.

[3] Angell on Highways, § 340.

[4] Wayde *v.* Carr, 2 Dow. & Ry. 255.

whatever part he fancies:[1] and in the crowded streets of a city situations and circumstances may frequently arise, where a deviation will not only be justifiable, but absolutely necessary.[2] And, of course, one may pass on the left side of a road, or across it, in order to stop on that side;[3] and conveyances stationary may be on either side."[4]

"I believe that if there was sufficient room for a defendant to pass without inconvenience, it will not assist him when sued to say that the plaintiff was on the wrong side.[5] Mr. Angell tells us that if a man, not on his own side, suddenly meets another and an injury results, he who is voluntarily in the wrong must answer for all damages, unless the other individual could have avoided the accident.[6] And the fact that the one on the wrong side is not able to turn out will not avail him as a defence."[7]

"Of course not. The injured one has not only to show that the injurer was on the wrong side, but also that he himself exercised ordinary precaution to avoid collision.[8] If my share of the road is trenched upon I cannot recklessly run into the

1 Aston *v.* Heaven, 2 Esp. 533; Palmer *v.* Barker, 11 Me. 338; Foster *v.* Goddard, 40 Me. 64.

2 Turley *v.* Thomas, 8 C. & P. 103.

3 Angell on Highways, § 336.

4 Johnson *v.* Small, 5 B. Mon. (Ken.), 25.

5 Clay *v.* Wood, 5 Esp. 44; Parker *v.* Adams, 12 Metc. 415; Kennard *v.* Burton, 11 Shepley (Me.), 39.

6 Angell, § 337.

7 Brooks *v.* Hart, 14 N. H. 307.

8 Parker *v.* Adams, *supra.*

trespasser, and then turn round and sue for injury arising from my devil-may-care conduct. I may, of course, try to pass, if passing is reasonably prudent; if not, I ought to delay and seek redress at law, if damage ensue from my detention.[1] If a wagon comes along so heavily laden that I cannot pass it, the driver should stop at a convenient place to let me go by.[2] A man on foot, or on horseback, or in a light trap, cannot insist upon a teamster with a heavy load giving up part of the beaten track, if there be sufficient room to pass without his doing so." [3]

"I believe," I said, "that in winter when the proper road is covered with snow, and the beaten track is at the side, persons meeting on it must turn to the right." [4]

"If a collision does take place," said Smith, who talked as if he had inwardly digested all the reports ever published, "through a defendant's fault, the plaintiff may recover against him damages commensurate with the whole of the injury sustained.[5] And, by-the-by, I noticed the other day, that the laws of the road do not apply to buildings which are traversing the highway." [6]

"I should think not," I replied.

A pause for a few minutes took place. Better

[1] Brooks *v.* Hart, 14 N. H. 307.
[2] Kennard *v.* Burton, 25 Me. 39.
[3] Grier *v.* Sampson, 27 Penn. St. 183.
[4] Jaquith *v.* Richardson, 8 Met. 213; Smith *v.* Dygert, 12 Barb. 613.
[5] Gilberton *v.* Richardson, 5 C. B. 502.
[6] Graves *v.* Shattuck, 35 N. H. 257

far for me if it had never been broken on that day. But it was ordained otherwise.

"Well," said Mr. Smith at length, "we have had a very pleasant drive together, and a very interesting conversation. I have enjoyed myself very much, for it is not very often that one can meet on the top of a coach, in this Ultima Thule of civilization, with a man who can discourse so learnedly on the law of carriers as you have done. But I regret to say that I must leave you at this little tavern, where the stage stops for dinner."

"I share your regret fully, and I, too, have thoroughly enjoyed myself, and even my bruised toe has forgotten to twinge and throb during our converse."

"By the way," added Smith, "I find I have forgotten, or lost, my purse; could you kindly lend me a V., for I have my fare to pay."

"Oh, certainly," I replied, with apparent pleasure, but with inward heaviness, for alas

> I could plead, expound and argue,
> Fire with wit, with wisdom glow;
> But one word for ever failed me,
> Source of all my pain and woe;
> Luckless man! I could not say it,
> Could not — dare not — answer: No!

The transfer of the Five was speedily made, and at that moment the driver reined in his old horses and drew up at the door of a country inn. Quickly my debtor jumped off the coach; with his bag swinging in his hand, a nod to me and a low salaam to the ladies, he was walking away, when the driver called after him: —

"I say, mister, where 's that ere fare?"

"Ah! that 's a trifle that quite escaped my memory," responded my quondam comrade. "Never mind, however, you will have a lien upon my trunk in the meantime." [1]

"Where 's your box?" queried Jehu.

"Oh! that 's a question more easily asked than answered. It is where many a more valuable thing is, *in nubibus*, or *in partibus infidelium.* However, it matters little, because you could not detain me for the paltry fare, nor the clothes that I have on, nor even this bag that I have in my manual possession.[2] So by-by to you."

And away he went, leaving coachee pouring forth his vials of wrath in epithets and expletives strong, if not polite.

"Alas," thought I to myself, "it is such sharp and improper conduct that makes men wish, like Shakespeare's Dick, 'to kill all the lawyers;' makes them abuse those who are (or should be) the counsellors, secretaries, interpreters, and servants of Justice — the lady and queen of all moral virtues — and apply to the members of our profession the language of Congreve of old: 'There 's many a cranny and leak unstopped in your conscience. If so be one had a pump in your bosom,

1 Wolf *v.* Summers, 2 Camp. 631.
2 Sunbolf *v.* Alford, 3 M. & W. 248.

we should discover a foul hold. They say a witch will sail in a sieve, but the devil could not venture aboard your conscience.' But I can flatter myself that an honest lawyer, like myself, 'is the life-guard of people's fortunes; the best collateral security for their estate; a trusty pilot to steer one through the dangerous and, oftentimes, inevitable ocean of contention; a true priest of justice, that neither sacrifices to fraud or covetousness; and one who can make people honest that are sermon proof.' He is one who can

> Make the cunning artless, tame the rude,
> Subdue the haughty, shake the undaunted soul;
> Yea, put a bridle in the lion's mouth,
> And lead him forth as a domestic cur."

CHAPTER VI.

DINING, RAINING, LOSING, AND ENDING.

Must wait at Stopping-places. — Place booked taken at any Time. — Falling in ascending. — Drenched with Rain. — Coachmen are Common Carriers, and liable as such. — Loss of Money. — Loss of Luggage. — Dangerous Short Cut. — Bridges. — Safe Arrival.

THE driver, annoyed at the loss of his fare, said he would drive ahead at once and not wait, as he usually did at this place, for his passengers to take refreshments, but as my wife was hungry and the old maids thirsty, I insisted upon his remaining; for a carrier has no right to deviate from established usages to gratify his own whims and fancies.[1] While we were partaking of a cold collation, portions of which, doubtless, had done duty on several former occasions, a gentleman arrived at the inn, and from his conversation with the driver I quickly perceived that he had paid his fare for the whole way from town to our journey's end, and that he now intended to take his seat, as he clearly had a right to do.[2] He, too, was booked for an inside place, and protested strongly because sufficient room had not been left for him, saying that as more than the legal number were

[1] Chitty on Carriers, 253; Story on Bailments, § 597.
[2] Ker *v.* Mountain, 1 Esp. 27.

already on board, he would not get on but would sue the proprietor for all expenses he might be put to in performing the remainder of his journey by another conveyance.[1]

"I took my place," he exclaimed with emphasis, "and now you are going to try to squeeze six people into an infernal box that only holds five. I 'll take a post-chaise and bring an action for all the expenses incurred. I 've paid my fare. It won't do; I told the clerk when I took my place that it would not do. I know these things have been done. I know they are done every day; but *I* never was done, and I never will be. Those who know me best know it; crush me."[2]

The son of Nimshi tried to smooth down matters, but in vain; and the irascible gent went off in high dudgeon; whereat I rejoiced.

Just as we were starting, an old woman approached, and after some chaffering agreed with the driver as to the sum for which he would carry her to the next village, and began to mount. Before she was up the horses started, and she was thrown to the ground and injured so much that she could not come with us. I endeavored to apply some balm by informing her that she had better sue the owner of the stage; for, she, being a passenger as soon as the contract was made, he was liable to her for the negligence of his man.[3]

[1] Chitty on Carriers, 252.
[2] See Mr. Dowler's remarks in Pickwick.
[3] Brien *v.* Bennett, 8 C. & P. 724; Lygo v. Newbold, 9 Ex. 302.

We had not gone far, after our refreshments, before the sky grew overcast, the wind arose, heavy clouds began to scud across the sky, distant mutterings of thunder grew more and more audible, rolling, rumbling, rattling, nearer and nearer, the heavens were wrapt in gloom, through which, ever and anon, the lightning flashed vividly. Quickly the thunderstorm was upon us, the rain descended first in large heavy drops, then in a perfect deluge; the sky seemed on fire with electric flashes, darting hither and thither like fiery, flying serpents. In vain the coachee whipped up his wearied horses and made their very bones to rattle, striving to gain shelter from the pitiless storm. Before protection could be gained we were all drenched to the epidermis; even those within did not escape, for the old stage leaked like a sieve and let in the flood at every part. (My wife declared afterwards that she had read that in the days of Henry II., of France, there were three, and only three, coaches in existence, one belonging to Catherine de Medicis, another to the fair, but frail, Diana of Poictiers, and the third to René de Laval, a noble seigneur, and that she verily believed that this was the one owned by the fat old René, so weak, so frail, so rickety, was the old antediluvian monster; in fact, she remarked, there was nothing strong about the entire concern except the smell!)

But, after all, it was only a thunderstorm, and

ere very long its fury was overpassed, the sun emerged from behind the murky clouds, and we all steamed away beneath its fiery rays like small portable steam-engines. Far worse, however, than being thoroughly damped ourselves, the heavy down-pour had penetrated our trunks and bags, playing the mischief with the things therein, for the carrier had not provided tarpaulins, or cart clothes and such necessary coverings to protect the baggage from the rain, as he was bound to do.[1] The thoughts of the damages which I might recover, alone kept me from pouring forth my ire upon the coachman's devoted head.

Of course, proprietors of stage-coaches,[2] or mail-coaches,[3] who hold themselves out as carriers of goods, as well as of passengers, are liable as common carriers, and responsible at common law for all damage and loss to goods during the carriage from what cause soever arising, save only the act of God; and this liability extends to the luggage of passengers, as well as to the goods of strangers, although no specific charge be made for the luggage.[4] In England (by the Railway Clauses Act) railways, stage-coach proprietors, and other common carriers of passengers, their baggage and

1 Webb *v.* Page, 6 M. & G. 204; Walker *v.* Jackson, 10 M. & W. 168; Phillco *v.* Sandford, 17 Texas, 227.

2 Clark *v.* Gray, 4 Esp. 177; Lovett *v.* Hobbs, 2 Shower, 127; Hutton *v.* Bolton, 1 H. Bla. 299 n.; Dwight *v.* Brewster, 1 Pickering (Mass.), 50; Jones *v* Voorhees, 10 Ohio, 145.

3 White *v.* Bolton, Peake, N. P. 113.

4 Robinson *v.* Dunmore, 2 B. & P. 416.

freight, are put upon precisely the same ground, both as to liability and as to any protection, privilege or exemption; and the same rule obtains in the great republic, except, perhaps, that inasmuch as transportation by rail is infinitely more perilous, a proportionate degree of watchfulness is demanded of carriers thereby. Care and diligence are relative terms, and the degree of care and watchfulness is to be increased in proportion to the hazard of the business.[1]

The thorough damping which he had received seemed to have had a mollifying effect upon our knight of the reins, and when I ventured to address him on the subject of his master's liability for loss or damage to luggage, I found him quite thawed out, in fact, communicative.

"Wal," said he, "I knows summat about that; but I rather guess you'd find yourself mistook if you thought him liable for all losses, and put a lot of money in your trunk, and did n't tell on it, and had it lost."

"Why," queried I, "what about that?"

"Not much, only this: a chap one time thought so as how he'd come a sharp dodge on a coachman, so he just put $11,250 in his old trunk and said nothing about it; and when they got to their journey's end the box was nowheres; the man tried to make the owner of the stage pay, but the judge decided he could not."

[1] Commonwealth *v.* Power, 7 Met. 601; Jencks *v.* Coleman, 2 Sumner, 221.

"Who told you all that?"

"Wal, stranger, I heerd it in rather a round-about way; my master told me, another man told him, and an angel told the other man."[1]

"Ah, indeed!" I exclaimed, "that is undoubted authority."

"Another time there was a *long fellow* put a £50 note in his bag among his old duds. In getting on the stage he gave his bag to the driver, who lost it; he sued the master to court, but the jury only paid him for his old clothes."[2]

"There must have been some stage-coachman on that jury," I said.

"Like enough; there's a deal of them scattered around every civilized country."

"I suppose you know," I added, "that if you were to carry parcels for your own particular profit, your master would not be liable for the loss of them,[3] unless, indeed, he paid you less wages, because of the opportunity thus afforded you of making small sums."[4]

"I guess there's no chance of my makin' a fortun', along this ere road that ere way. Folks think I ought to carry their traps for nothing. Look ye here, mister, how would it be 'sposing a man took his portmantee with him, and kept his own eye on til it, and it was lost after all."

[1] Angell on Carriers, 262.
[2] Miles *v.* Cottle, 4 M. & P. 630; 6 Bing. 743; and on this point see chapter 8.
[3] Butter *v.* Basing, 2 C. & P. 614.
[4] Dwight *v.* Brewster, 1 Pick. (Mass.), 50.

"Oh, it's clear the owner of the coach would be liable.[1] But if a gentleman keep, for instance, his overcoat wholly in his own custody and possession, and does not actually deliver it to the carrier, the latter cannot reasonably be held liable for the loss[2] if it disappears."

(P. S. and N. B. Any person or persons desirous of becoming thoroughly posted upon the all important question of the liability of carriers for the loss of baggage, will find it to their advantage to consult chapter fifteen of this my book.)

"I say, mister, had I better take a short cut over that ere bridge, which is so rotten that I calkerlate it will go down mighty soon with a tremendous whack into the water below, or go away round a couple of miles to the stone bridge?" queried the driver.

"Well," I replied, "I think you had better go round, for the law saith, if a common carrier — which you decidedly are in every sense of the word — goes by ways that be dangerous, or drive by night, or in other inconvenient times, or if he overcharge a horse, whereby he falleth into water or otherwise, so that the stuff is hurt or impaired, then he shall be charged for his misdemeanor."[3]

"But why does not the corporation repair the bridge?" I added.

"Oh, they don't own it; old Squire Squaretoes

1 Robinson v. Dunmore, 2 B. & P. 419; Brooke v. Pickwick, 4 Bing. 218.

2 Tower v. Utica & Sch. Rw., 7 Hill, 47.

3 Doctor & Stud., Dial. 2d, p. 224.

built it and owns it; but he lets folks cross it if they choose," replied the man.

"Then it is clear we would have no one to sue if any accident happened through its defective state."[1]

I trust that my readers (if I have any) will understand that a town is not liable for injuries caused by a bridge being out of repair, if it has become so, suddenly and unexpectedly, by reason of a freshet, and sufficient time has not elapsed to enable the authorities to repair it, or to guard travellers against the danger;[2] but if the chairman of the board of supervisors has had notice of the defect, and no proper precautions are taken to guard against accidents, the town will be held liable for negligence.[3]

Quickly now we drove along the bank of a little babbling, bubbling river, which "like a silver thread with sunsets strung upon it thick like pearls" wound in and out, and round about, doubling the distance we had to travel; but I was quite content and sought not to descend from my high perch, for the breeze was

> "'Sweet as Sabæan odors from the shores
> Of Araby the blest;'

and the woods near by had many verdurous glooms and winding mossy ways, to charm the eye, and I had ever loved to gaze upon

1 Gautret *v.* Egerton, L. R. 2 C. P. 371; State *v.* Seawell, 3 Hawks, 193.

2 Jaquish *v.* Ithaca, 36 Wis. 108; Ward *v.* Jefferson, 24 Wis. 342.

3 Ibid.

"groups of lovely elm-trees bending
Languidly their leaf-crowned heads,
Like youthful maids, when sleep descending,
Warns them to their silken beds."

On and on we clattered along the rough and stony road, rattling and jolting, till a loud and sharp "Toot-toot-toot," with a long clear flourish "that warbled away in an acoustic ringlet" from the driver's horn, announced the fact that that day's work was done; that our journey was complete, and we were safe in the little village of Ayr.

As our journey beyond this point was upon the trackless deep, I will here say nothing about it, save that we were while on board the steamboats neither blown up nor drowned.

CHAPTER VII.

STATIONS AND STARTING.

Meditations on Crossings. — Bell or Whistle. — People on Track. — Access to Stations. — Slippery Ice. — Checks on Trunks. — Notice of Arrivals and Departures. — Trains late as usual. — Must keep Time. — Damages, Damages. — Proof. — Ill fared Welfare. — Waiting-rooms not Smoke-houses. — Charge of the Iron Horse. — Tripped up.

In course of time I had to go off on business, and, notwithstanding the unhappy demise of my wife's step-mother's brother's wife's mother's aunt, I resolved to patronize the cars, and having long before settled the insurance question to my own satisfaction, I purchased both a railway and an accident ticket, and as the proper hour for the departure of my train approached, started bag in hand, being minded to go afoot to the station. "As I walked by myself, I talked to myself and myself replied to me, and the questions myself then put to myself with the answers, I give thee," my would-be-wise reader.

Coming upon the railroad where it ran close to a house which hid the line on one side completely from view, I was rather startled by a freight-train dashing past within a few feet of my nose, and I asked myself: "Should not a bell have been rung?" and I replied: "Yes, wherever a train crosses a highway there the bell should be rung or the whistle sounded;[1] and no engine should have gone at such a speed." "Should not the company place a watchman at a crossing to warn pedestrians of the approach of trains?" the answer that came was, "I fancy not, for *primâ facie*, a foot-passenger crossing a railway is bound to look out for his own safety;[2] just as it is his duty to use due care and caution in crossing a street, so as not recklessly to get among the carriages."[3] There is, it appears, no general duty devolving upon railway companies to place watchmen at such places, but it depends upon the particular circumstances of each individual case as to whether the omission of such a precaution amounts to negligence or not.[4] If, however, one is employed, his neglect of duty will make the company liable.[5]

But then this crossing, I thought, is peculiarly dangerous, the line being hid as it is? In such a case the mere occurrence of an accident to one crossing will be evidence of negligence.[6] If a railroad unnecessarily crosses a highway in such a manner and place that travellers can neither see

1 Galena & Chi. Rw. *v.* Loomis, 13 Ill. 548.

2 Skelton *v.* L. & N. W. Rw., L. R, 2 C. P. 631; Boggs *v.* Great Western Rw., 23 U. C. C. P. 573.

3 Williams *v.* Richards, 3 C. & K. 82; Cotton *v* Wood, 8 C. B. (N. S.), 571.

4 Stubley *v.* L. & N. W. Rw., L. R., 1 Ex. 13.

5 Kissenger *v.* N. Y., etc., Rw., 56 N. Y. 538.

6 Bilbee *v.* L. & B. Rw., 18 C. B. (N. S.), 584; see also, Stapley *v.* L. B. & S. C. Rw., L. R., 1 Ex. 21.

nor hear an approaching train until too late to save themselves; or if a company erect a building so as to shut off the view, they will be liable for collisions, in the absence of negligence on the part of the injured ones.[1] I remember that once, on a certain foggy morning in the land of fogs, a man took the trouble to look up the line and to look down the line, but owing to the dimness of the light failed to see a train coming; the engine never whistled, the man was injured and the company was found guilty of negligence.[2] Where persons are in the habit of crossing a line at a particular place, though there is no right of way there, still the responsibility of taking reasonable precautions in their use of such place is thrown upon the company.[3]

The omission to give the signals required by statute, such as, ringing the bell or sounding the whistle, constitutes a *primâ facie* case of negligence; still, to make the company liable for damages, the injury must be the result of the want of the signal, and the onus of showing this will not be upon the company, but upon the plaintiff.[4]

The public has a right to presume that if the proper warnings are not given at a crossing, that the speed of the train will be reduced; if not, to

1 Mackay *v.* N. Y. C., 35 N. Y. 75; Richardson *v.* N. Y. C., 45 N. Y. 846.

2 James *v.* Gt W. Rw., L. R., 2 C. P. 634 n.; see p. 63.

3 Barrett *v.* Midland Rw., 1 F. & F. 361.

4 Galena, etc., Union Rw. *v.* Loomis, 13 Ill. 548; Wakefield *v.* C. & P. R. Rw., 37 Vt. 330.

prevent an injured one getting damage it must be proved that he was rash. The company will be liable if he kept a proper lookout, though he was incautious in going on the track.[1]

Every one attempting to cross a railroad should do it with his eyes open. He should listen for the signals, notice all the signs that may be put up as warnings, and look up and down the road.[2] If, however, he is driving across, it does not appear that he is bound to get out of his carriage, or even stop for the purpose of listening.[3] If, by the use of one's optics, the train could have been perceived, it is presumed in case of a collision, that the man hurt did not look, or did not heed, and so under ordinary circumstances, the company will not be liable.[4] Contributory negligence on the part of the afflicted excuses the railroad, whether the proper signals have been given or not, or whether the company is guilty of any other negligence or not.[5]

When a carriage-way crossed a line on the level, and the gates on the down side of the line being open, young Wanless, with some other boys, entered on the railway at the time when a train on the up side was passing, intending to cross as soon as the train had passed; meanwhile another train,

1 B. & O. Rw. *v.* Trainor, 33 Md. 542; Cliff *v.* Midland Rw., L. R., 5 Q. B. 258.

2 Wharton on Neg. § 382 and notes.

3 Davis *v.* N. Y. C., 47 N. Y. 400.

4 Wharton, § 382.

5 Ernst *v.* Hudson R Rw., 39 N. Y. 61.

on the down side, which he could have seen if he had looked, knocked him down and injured him. The Court of Queen's Bench and the House of Lords both held that the company were guilty of negligence;[1] and that having the gate open was an intimation to the public that the line was clear. However, in New York State it was decided that a similar breach of duty only gave a right to the penalty affixed thereto, and was not evidence of negligence:[2] and that one must keep a lookout, even though no danger signal is given.[3] On the other hand, other American cases hold that one has a right to expect a company to do its duty, and give the proper notices and warnings.[4]

When on the point of crossing a track about the time a train is due one should not bundle up his head, so as to impair the sense of hearing, and then go straight ahead without looking out for the cars. If a man does so and is made mince-meat of, he has only himself to blame, even though neither bell nor whistle sounded.[5] One must not even hold his hat on with his hand on a rainy, blowy, stormy, snowy night, if he is thereby prevented seeing an approaching train.[6]

1 Wanless *v.* N. E. Rw., L. R., 6 Q. B. 481; *S. C.*, L. R., 7 E. & I. App. 12; Stapley *v.* London & B. Rw., L. R., 1 Ex. 21.

2 Brown *v.* Buffalo, etc , 22 N. Y. 191.

3 Havens *v.* Erie Rw., 41 N. Y. 296.

4 Hart *v.* Erie Rw., 3 Alb. L. J. 312; Tabor *v.* Mo. Vall. Rw., 46 Mo. 353; *S. C.*, 2 Am. Rep. 270.

5 Steves *v.* Oswego & S. Rw., 18 N. Y. 422; Wilds *v.* Hudson R. Rw.. 24 N. Y. 430; but see Chaffee *v.* Boston & L. Rw., 104 Mass. 108.

6 Butterfield *v.* Western Rw., 10 Allen, 532; Miller *v* G. T. R., 25 C. P. (Ont.), 389.

A railway company is not bound to use the same amount of care towards strangers who voluntarily and wilfully go on their track as they owe towards their passengers. This, Mr. Brand found out after he had his legs cut off while walking on the track through the city.[1] If one is unlawfully on the track, or contributes to the injury by his own carelessness or negligence, yet if the injury could have been avoided by the company's servants using ordinary care, the railway is liable for damages.[2] An engine driver, however, is not bound to slacken speed when he sees before him, on the track, one whom he may reasonably suppose can take care of himself, until he sees that otherwise the man, woman, or child will be run over; but it is his duty to check the train so soon as he spies a very young child, or apparently helpless person in the way; if he does not do so and a collision ensues, the company will be liable for the consequences.[3]

A company is bound so to lay their line at a crossing that no injury will be done by reason of the rails being above the level of the road.[4]

Near the station and forming one way of access thereto is a bridge, said to be in a dangerous state,

[1] Brand *v.* Troy & S. Rw., 8 Barb. 368; Anderson *v.* N. Rw., 25 C. P. (Ont.), 301.

[2] Brown *v.* Hannibal & St. J., etc., 50 Mo. 461; B. & O. Rw. *v.* Trainor, 33 Md. 542.

[3] Lake Shore Rw. *v.* Miller, 25 Mich. 277; Telfer *v.* N. Rw., 30 N. J. 188; St. Louis, etc., *v.* Manly, 58 Ill. 300.

[4] Oliver *v.* N. E. Rw., L. R., 9 Q. B. 409; Thompson *v.* G. W. R., 24 C. P. (Ont.), 429.

and across this I saw several persons hurrying, but I preferred to go round by a longer way, for although it has been decided that a company is liable for the death of a passenger through the faulty construction of a bridge erected by them for the more convenient access to the station, when there is a safe one about one hundred yards further off which the unfortunate deceased might have used,[1] still I considered discretion the better part of valor and chose keeping sound bones in a whole skin to my wife enjoying plenty and prosperity out of my life insurances. Besides, I recollected that Mr. Justice Clesby had once said, that where a passenger having full knowledge of the fact, still preferred using a dangerous way and in consequence was injured, it would seem that such a foolish body would have no ground of complaint, on the principle of the old maxim *volenti non fit injuria.*[2] What risks men will run to save a few minutes or a few steps; verily well saith the poet, —

> "Of all the creatures that fly in the air
> Swim in the sea, or tread earth so fair,
> From Paris and Rome to Peru and Japan,
> The most foolish beast, as I think, is man."

On entering the station-yard I found engines puffing and snorting, backing and switching on every side, and really it was at considerable danger of my journey being summarily put an end to ere well commenced, that I made my way to the plat-

[1] Longmore *v.* G. W. Rw., 19 C. B. (N. S.) 183.
[2] Bridges *v.* N. London, etc., L. R., 6 Q. B. 377.

form. This rather annoyed me and ruffled the habitual serenity of my temper (and the serenity of the most serene would be tried by a locomotive spirting and squirting out a jet of steam at one's nether garments), for it is the duty of railway companies to take all reasonable care to keep their premises in such a state that those whom they invite there (and they invite all who may desire to be carried to any place whither the line runs) will not be unduly exposed to danger.[1] But they need not go so far as to put a hand-rail upon a stairway for unsteady folks to steady themselves with, where the stair is protected on either side by walls; and they may put brass on the steps instead of lead, although it is more slippery.[2]

I had scarcely stepped on to the platform when one foot slipped from under me, and down with a whack I descended upon the back of my head; my carpet-bag, too, fell with a crash, telling of ruin to some valuable therein contained. Up rose I in wrath and found that a strip of ice had been the cause of my discomfiture, and I registered an oath on high that the company should answer to me in solid gold for the damages I had sustained; for I knew of one Shepherd, who having fallen on a slippery place, while he tramped up and down the platform waiting for a train, recovered a goodly sum from the company; and Martin, B.,

[1] Welfare *v.* London & Brighton Rw., L. R., 4 Q. B. 693; Stott *v.* G. T. R., 24 C. P. (Ont.), 347.

[2] Crafter *v.* Metropolitan Rw., L. R., 1 C. P. 300.

said, railway servants ought to be alert during cold weather to see whether there is ice upon the platform, and to remove it, or make it safe by sanding it, or otherwise, if it is there.[1]

On I strode in ire — for I saw some girls snickering at me — to where the baggage-master was checking the luggage.

"Check this," I exclaimed.

"Take it into the car with you," he replied.

"I won't; you must check it; there's a handle," I returned.

"I won't; handle be hanged; you must take it," he retorted.

"All right," I answered, inwardly resolving that as a check had been refused me when demanded, the company should pay me the penalty of eight dollars, as well as the costs of the action which I should bring against them for it, and that I would insist upon the conductor in charge of the train refunding me the fare that I had paid for my ticket.[2] I was sorry now that I had bought the ticket in advance, for under the circumstances they would have had no right to collect or receive from me any toll or fare.[2]

I was determined to teach railway companies their duties, and baggage-masters are far too fond of refusing to check small parcels or bags; and at way stations, in their wisdom, even decline some-

[1] Shepperd *v.* Midland Rw. Co., 20 W. R. 705; but see *ante*, p. 9.
[2] Railway Act, 1868, § 20, ss. 5 and 6 (Can.).

times to check large trunks, although the law of this Canada of ours says, "Checks shall be affixed by an agent or servant to every parcel of baggage having a handle, loop or fixture of any kind thereupon (though what may be included in the latter term goodness only knows), and a duplicate shall be given to the passenger delivering the same."[1]

It was not many minutes before I found cause of action number *three* against the respectable railway company to whose tender mercies I was about to commit my precious self. The law directs that "the trains shall be started and run at regular hours to be fixed by public notice,"[2] but most locomotives — their drivers and conductors — treat that clause with a contempt truly philosophical. The train by which I desired to embark was overdue for half an hour, according to the time-table which hung mockingly on the wall, so I looked about me to see if there had been "put up on the outside of the station-house over the platform of the station in some conspicuous place, a written or printed notice signed by the station-master, stating to the best of his knowledge and belief the time when such over-due train might be expected to reach the station," as it was the duty of the company to do. Of course, no such notice was visible, such enactments being too often deemed effete from the very day they appear on

[1] Railway Act, 1868, § 20, s. 5.
[2] Ibid. § 20, s. 2.

the statute book, so I still further comforted and consoled my wounded feelings by the thought that for this neglect or omission they were liable to an action at my suit, in which full costs might be recovered[1] (the latter was an object of importance just now).

I now retired into the waiting-room to ponder over the business that had thus unexpectedly turned up. I knew that few men were bold enough to fight a great railway company on any question, and especially one involving a small amount, and that as a result of this railways have been virtually exempt from the penalties attaching to many breaches of duty and of contract which they are daily committing; but I determined to sacrifice myself for the good of my fellows. I was eager, too, to see my name figuring in the reports.

I also now began to reflect that if the train was much later, I would miss my appointments, and then cause of action number *four* would accrue. For it is as clear as daylight that if a railway company publishes or authorizes the publication of a time-table, representing that a train will start at a particular hour for a particular place, or arrive at a particular hour, and through negligence no train is prepared or arrives, the company is responsible in damages to all persons who have acted upon the faith of the representation, and have been deceived and put to expense, and have sustained

[1] 34 Vict. c. 43, § 6 (Can.).

damage thereby;[1] but if they give proper notice they will not be liable for any necessary delay.[2] A company announced that their trains would be punctual as far as possible; though, they said, they did not undertake that they would run exactly according to the time-tables, and that they would not be liable for any loss or damage arising from unpunctuality; the court, however, held, that a delay of twenty-seven minutes *en route* between Liverpool and Leeds was evidence of negligence or want of reasonable efforts to be punctual.[3] A notice that a company will not be responsible for deviations from the time-tables, unless the detentions are caused by the wilful neglect of their employees, is practically invalid.[4] The company make a continuous representation whilst they continue to hold out printed or written papers as being their time-tables, and they thereby make a public profession and representation that they will exercise their vocation of common carriers, and dispatch passengers or goods, as the case may be, to certain specified places at or about the time named in such tables; and if they fail to do so they commit a breach of their duty as common carriers, and are guilty of a fraudulent representation, which may be the foundation of an action for deceit by any one who, relying on the

[1] Addison on Torts, 3d ed. 447.
[2] Redfield on Rail., vol. ii., p. 276.
[3] Le Blanche *v.* L. & N. W. Rw., 34 L. T. R. 25.
[4] Becke *v.* G. W. R., 18 Sol. J. 972.

representation, tenders himself or his goods for conveyance at the appointed time, and finds there is no train about to start.[1]

Though neither time-table nor advertisement is an actual warranty for the arrival and departure of trains at the time named, still companies are unquestionably liable for any want of punctuality which they could have avoided by the use of due care or skill; nor can they plead any excuse, the existence of which was known to them when the tables were published.[2] And when there has been a change of time, due care should be used in notifying the public.[3]

I also ran the risk of missing the connection at B.; but I remembered that once upon a time a tailor going down into the country to measure his customers, in consequence of the train not having reached a junction at the time advertised, missed his connection and had to spend the night at the junction and pay extra fare the next morning; he sued the company and recovered the amount of his hotel expenses and the extra fare, but not for damages sustained by not reaching his customers at the appointed time [but this rule seems to be almost equivalent to a denial of all beneficial redress in such cases.[4]] The chief baron in giving

1 Denton *v.* G. N. Rw., 5 Ell. & Bl. 860; *In re* Oxlade, 1 C. B. (N. S.), 454; Heirn *v.* McCaughan, 32 Miss. 17.

2 Gordon *v.* M. & L. Rw., 52 N. H. 596.

3 Sears *v.* Eastern Rw., 14 Allen, 433.

4 Redfield on Railways, vol. ii., p 277 n.

judgment, stated that as a rule, generally in actions upon contracts the plaintiff is entitled to recover whatever damage naturally results from the breach of the contract, but not damages for the disappointment of mind occasioned by the breach of contract.[1] When in consequence of the company's negligence M. Le Blanche reached Leeds too late for the Scarborough train, and he took a special train whereby he reached Scarborough an hour earlier than if he had waited for the next regular train, the court considered that although he had no special business at S., yet still he was entitled to recover from the railroad authorities the cost of the special train. But a man should not take a special, hoping to have the expense recouped him, unless it is a reasonable thing to do under the circumstances.[2] In Manchester (England), a music teacher recovered against a railway company five shillings which he had had to pay for cab-hire, the train through delays having failed to make certain connections.[3] If a party bound to do a certain thing does not do so, the other party may do it for him as reasonably and nearly as may be, and charge him for the reasonable expenses incurred in doing so. A company cannot escape damages for its failure to carry a passenger

[1] Hamlin *v.* G. N. R., 1 H. & N. 408, and as to damages for remote and collateral consequences, see Story *v.* N. Y. & H. Rw., 2 Selden, 85; Horner *v.* Wood, 16 Barb. 386.

[2] Le Blanche *v.* L. & N. W. R., 34 L. T. R. 25; reversed on Appeal, W. Notes, May 27, 1876.

[3] Becker *v.* L. & N. W. Rw., cited in 10 C. L. J. 311.

with sufficient dispatch by the fact that the delay was the wilful act of the conductor in charge of the train.[1] It must clearly appear that the damages were sustained without any fault on the part of the traveller, and in spite of his utmost efforts to avoid them.[2]

The mere production of a ticket, however, is not sufficient evidence of a contract to carry a passenger to a certain place within a given time, as one Hurst discovered when he sued for various expenses and losses sustained through missing a certain train in consequence of delay in starting; the time-table must be produced to prove the contract.[3] And as I knew that to prove that the table was issued by authority I would have to show either that it was bought at one of the company's stations, or at one of their recognized receiving offices, or that it was posted up in some office or place where the advertisements of the company were usually placed,[4] I started off on a tour of investigation to see if I could pick up the desired article, or evidence that would answer my purpose, keeping in mind how ill fared my friend, Mr. Welfare. He once innocently inquired of a railway porter when the train would be in, and being referred by the official to a time-table hanging upon the wall, he went to consult it; while

1 Weed *v.* P. R. Rw., 17 N. Y. 362.

2 Benson *v.* New Jersey Rw. Co., 9 Bosw. 412.

3 Hurst *v.* Gt. Western Rw., 34 L. J. C. P. 265; Robinson *v.* The same, 35 L. J. C. P. 123.

4 Addison on Torts, p. 487.

doing so, down tumbled, through a hole in the roof, a heavy plank and a roll of zinc, and smote Mr. Welfare on the neck, doing him grievous bodily harm; glancing upwards, the poor stricken one beheld the legs of a man upon the roof. Yet for the damages done the company was held not liable, as for aught that my friend showed at the trial the man might have been the servant of a contractor employed to mend the roof, or the misfortune might have been the result of a pure accident.[1] So the sufferings of my friend served but to point a moral — Beware! — and to adorn a volume of reports.

But to return from this digression anent my friend, to the topic on which I was musing. Draper, C. J., in one case, held that a time-table could not be treated as a part of the contract, but amounted to a representation only; and that to recover damages one would have to show that he bought his ticket before the time specified for the train leaving, and not merely before the arrival of the train, for if that were after the time specified, the would-be passenger would know as well as the company that the time-table had been departed from.[2]

While I was thus deeply ruminating, an old friend appeared, — a Q. C., of high standing, at the bar of a neighboring city, — and we went outside to enjoy a chat and weed while waiting for

[1] Welfare *v.* London & Brighton Rw. Co., L. R., 4 Q. B. 693.

[2] Briggs *v.* Grand Trunk Rw. Co., 24 U. C. Q. B. 510, 516.

the train. Seeing an elderly female turn up her nose as a whiff of smoke tickled her nostrils, as if it were in very deed a blast from the lower regions, as King James said it wăs, my friend remarked: —

"Did you see that decision of Dillon, C. J., where he held that a woman who found the waiting-room unfit for her occupation — tobacco and other impurities being offensive to her delicate nerves — and so attempted to enter the cars which had not as yet come up to the platform, and was injured by the giving way of the platform steps, was entitled to recover?"[1]

"No," I replied.

"He ruled that it is the duty of railway passenger carriers to provide comfortable rooms for the accommodation of passengers while waiting at the stations, and to enforce such regulations in regard to smoking therein as to enable persons to occupy them in reasonable comfort."

"A very good decision for the ladies and those who have to wait hour after hour in a dirty room for a train ages behind its time."

"Still I think it is pushing the doctrine of the liability of companies rather far."

"Yes," I returned, "and rather in the teeth of the dictum of Mr. Justice Hannan, in Siner *v.* Great Western,[2] where he said he thought that

[1] McDonald *et ux.* *v.* Chicago & N. W. R. Co., 26 Iowa, 124.
[2] L. R., 3 Exch. 150.

juries took an exaggerated view of the duties of railway companies; that the companies have done so much for the comfort and convenience of travellers that it is now made the subject of complaint if the highest degree of luxurious care is not attained in all their arrangements."

"His is a much more sensible view of the case," said Smith, who held some railway shares, "and one more likely to produce dividends for unfortunate stock-holders. If people avail themselves of the benefits of railway travellers, they should make some allowances. Ah! look at our fair friend!"

She was at the far end of the platform, and an engine attached to a freight train seemed to be rushing straight at her; she turned and fled, with a scream, to avoid the charge of the iron horse, and in her hurry tripped over a barrow and fell prostrate. The career of the locomotive was stopped. It appeared that its antics had been caused by the negligent displacement of a switch. We raised the lady and found that although slightly damaged she was more frightened than hurt. We consoled her with the assurance that if she chose to sue the company she could make them pay for the elephantine gambols of the fiery steed which had so disturbed her equanimity.[1]

Seeing a man a short way off to whom I desired to speak, I was on the point of jumping down off the platform, when my Q. C. exclaimed: —

[1] Caswell v. Boston & Worcester Rw., 98 Mass. 194.

"Hold! be not rash! If you jump, instead of going down by the steps, and are hurt, you can never make the company pay for the plasters and the salves;[1] besides here 's the train."

And so indeed it was at last. Up it thundered to the station amid screeching and bell-ringing: out rushed the passengers eager to reach the refreshment room. The crowd pushed my chum against a portable weighing-machine, and, catching his foot in it, he fell and injured himself. Seeing that he was not very seriously damaged I could not help crying out: —

"Hold! be not rash! I knew a case on all fours with yours, where the foot of a machine projected above the level of the platform six inches and was unfenced; there it had stood for years without doing any damage, and it was held that there was no evidence to go to a jury of any negligence, the machine being where it might have been seen, and the accident not being one which could have been reasonably anticipated.[2] An exactly similar case. Ho! ho! ho!"

"I wish the whole platform had given way with the weight of that mob, and then there would without doubt have been evidence of negligence. Besides I might have had the pleasure of seeing you break your leg;" testily replied the Q. C. And he added, and more correctly

1 Forsyth *v.* Boston & Alb. Rw., 103 Mass. 510.

2 Cornman *v.* Eastern Counties Rw., 4 H. & N. 781; see also Blackman *v.* London, B., & S. C. Rw., 17 W. R. 769.

than an angry man usually speaks, "A company should not allow their platform to be overcrowded, and they ought to have adequate means for protecting their passengers in the event of an unusual influx of travellers.[1] They are bound to see that the number of porters at each station is adequate for the safety of passengers." [2]

"Ah! my dear sir, one must be careful and walk circumspectly about a station. You know where a man fell, seriously hurting himself, on a staircase down which some forty thousand people had passed every month without an accident, the court held that there was no evidence of negligence on the part of the company to go to a jury, although the brass covering on the step had been worn smooth, and said that 'the mere fact of a man having fallen and hurt himself is not sufficient to charge the company with negligence in the construction of their station; and the court is in an especial manner bound to see that the evidence submitted to the jury in order to establish negligence, is sufficient and proper to go to them.'" [3]

[1] Hogan *v.* S. E. Rw., 28 L. T. (N. S.), 271.

[2] Jackson *v.* Metropolitan Rw. L. R. 10 C. P. 49.

[3] Crafter *v.* Metropolitan Rw. Co., L. R., 1 C. P. 300. Where on the platform there were two doors in close proximity to each other, the one for necessary purposes, had painted over it the words "For gentlemen," the other had over it "Lamp room." The plaintiff having occasion to go to the former, inquired its whereabouts and was directed to it; by mistake he opened the door of the lamp room, fell down some stairs, and was injured: *Held*, that in the absence of evidence that the place was more than ordinarily dangerous, a nonsuit was right. Toomey *v.* London B. & S. C., 3 C. B. (N. S.), 146.

CHAPTER VIII.

TICKETS.

Man and Wife double as to Baggage.—Money in Trunk.—Authority of American Decisions. — Annual Tickets. — Badge of Officers. — Legislature outwitted. — "Tickets, Sir." — "Good for this Day only." — "Good for this Trip." — Stepping off. – Lose a Ticket, and pay again. — The Acts.

JUST as we were starting, I overheard an altercation between the baggage-man and a woman of a rather masculine appearance, "with angular outlines and plain surface, hair like the fibrous covering of a cocoanut in gloss and suppleness as well as color, and a voice at once thin and strenuous — acidulous enough to produce effervescence with alkalies, and stridulous enough to sing duets with the katydids." He was asserting that she had too much baggage and that she must pay freight; the woman demurred to this, and protested that as she and her husband were travelling together they were entitled to a double quantity of luggage. In this she was clearly right, as, though the law considers that a man and a woman joined together in the bonds of wedlock are one, still as respects baggage they are two,[1] or half a dozen, if one may judge from Saratoga trunks.

[1] Great Northern Rw. *v.* Shepherd, 8 Ex. 30.

The disputants moved off and I did not hear the functionary's decision.

As my companion opened his pocket-book to put in his checks, I noticed that he had nothing therein except a few cents, so I remarked jokingly: —

"You don't appear to have much of the needful about you."

He replied, "Pshaw! I am not such a goose as to carry money in my pocket to afford the light-fingered gentry an opportunity of enriching themselves at my expense."

"But how do you manage to travel without money? I should like to learn the secret," I said.

"So should I. I carry my cash in my trunk."

"In your trunk! Suppose you lose it?"

"Well, the company 's liable," he replied.

"Should n't think so," I said.

"But I am sure of it. It has been held that common carriers of passengers are responsible for money *bonâ fide* included in the baggage of a passenger, for travelling purposes and personal use, to an amount not exceeding what a prudent man — like myself for instance — would deem proper and necessary for the purpose.[1] But they are not responsible for money beyond such an amount, or intended for other purposes, unless, of course, the loss is occasioned by the gross negligence of the carriers or their servants." [2]

[1] Jordan *v.* Fall River Rw., 5 Cush. 69.

[2] Orange County Bank *v.* Brown, 9 Wend. 85; Weed *v.* Saratoga & Sch. Rw., 19 Wend. 534; Duffy *v.* Thompson, 4 E. D. Smith, 178.

"Well, I don't think you are a prudent man; besides, I fancy that 's only an American authority," I remarked.

"Only an American authority! Suppose it is, it is not to be despised. Bramwell, B., once said, that although the American authorities are not indeed binding upon us, still they are entitled to respect as the opinions of professors of English law, and entitled to respect according to the position of those professors and the reasons they give for their opinions,[1] and Spragge, C., in a late case, uses a similar expression."[2]

"Of course I bow to the dictum of the learned baron and chancellor. But doubtless there are American cases the other way."

"Perhaps. In fact I know there are.[3] But the great American authority, Judge Redfield, thinks they are incorrect.[4] I can give you a Pennsylvania case sustaining the Massachusetts one I quoted; and that is where the company in their advertisements stated that passengers were prohibited from taking anything as baggage but wearing apparel, which would be at the risk of the owner, and the trunk of a passenger contained specie — the extra weight beyond the usual allowance was paid for and the company's agent took

[1] Osborn *v.* Gillett, L. R., 8 Ex. 92.

[2] Deedes *v.* Graham, 20 Grant, 258, 270.

[3] Grant *v.* Newton, 1 E. D. Smith, 95; Chicago and Aurora Rw. *v.* Thompson, 19 Ill. 578.

[4] Red on Railways, vol. ii., pp. 56–58.

charge of it. The trunk wandered from the right way, went astray and was lost; and it was held that it was not incumbent upon the passenger to inform the carrier of the contents of the trunk unless he was asked, and that it was immaterial whether it was to be considered baggage or freight, and that the company was liable for its loss through the negligence or fraud of their agents." [1]

"Well, such may be the law on the other side of the line, but in this hyperborean Dominion of ours I must say that I think it is somewhat different. I think that if the conduct of the traveller has in any way contributed to the loss, he has no ground at common law for demanding compensation from the carrier.[2] Why, there is that old case in Burrows where a prudent man like yourself hid £100 stg. in an old nail-bag with some hay, and gave it to a common carrier to be taken to a banker; the money was lost, but the carrier was held not responsible, as the consignor had neglected to tell him the exceeding value of the bag and so prevented him taking due care of it.[3] Then there was the case of the guineas tied up with a bit of string in a brown-paper parcel,[4] the case of the sovereigns in the tea,[5] and the bank-

[1] Camden & Amboy Rw. *v.* Baldauf, 16 Penn. St. (4 Harris), 67; see also Walker *v* Jackson, 10 M. & W. 161, as to not inquiring contents, and Crouch *v.* L. & N. W. Rw., 14 C. B. 255, as to right to inquire.

[2] Butterworth *v.* Brownlow, 34 L. J. C. P. 267.

[3] Gibbon *v.* Paynton, 4 Burr. 2298.

[4] Clay *v.* Willan, 1 H. B. 298.

[5] Bradley *v.* Waterhouse, 3 C. & P. 318.

notes and gold in the school-boy's box,[1] in all of which the carriers were held relieved from liability. Then in England there is the Carrier's Act (11 Geo. IV. and 1 Wm. IV., c. 68), applying to all goods above £10."[2]

Here I was interrupted by the sudden cry of "Tickets! Tickets!" which rang through the car. The conductor entered, and stopped in front of a gentleman who said: —

"I have not got my ticket here. I hold a season one."

"That won't do, sir;" said the man. "Holders of annual tickets travelling on the line are bound to produce their tickets as much as ordinary passengers.[3] So take your choice, show your ticket, pay your fare, or out you go."[4]

"Well," replied the gentleman, "sooner than be turned out with my baggage, wherever you in your wisdom should deem best, I will pay my fare."

"Don't do it, sir;" I almost without intending it called out, so eager was I in my crusade against the company, "the conductor has no right to demand the tickets, nor receive any fare, nor in fact can he exercise any of the powers of his office,

[1] Batson v. Donavan, 4 B. & Ald. 37.

[2] By it no carrier is liable for loss or injury to any articles of great value in small compass, or for money, bills, notes, jewelry, etc., above £10, unless the value and nature of the property has been declared, and an increased charge paid for it.

[3] Woodard v. Eastern Counties Rw., 7 Jur. (N. S.), 971, 4 L. T. (N. S.), 336; Downs v. N. Y. & N. H. Rw., 36 Conn. 287.

[4] Railway Act (Can.) 1868, § 20, s. 12.

or meddle or interfere with any passenger or his baggage unless he has upon his hat or cap a badge indicating his office ;[1] and a company before they can enforce any law as to the production of tickets must bring themselves strictly within the terms of the law."[2]

"Sold again!" cried the wretched official, as he lugged out from his coat pocket a small cap ornamented with the word "*Conductor*," and showing it to me he added, "You pretend to know a great deal about the law, so perhaps you recollect that the statute does not say that the cap or hat, with the badge, is to be worn on the head. The law in its wisdom assumed that officers of the company would or must have caps or hats, and that they would or must wear them, and wear them upon the head, but it did not enact that they should do so.[3] It never entered the wise noddles of the legislators at Ottawa that a man might own two caps, a jolly fur one for use, and another little chap for show."

"I acknowledge that I spoke with undue haste," I meekly replied, feeling very crestfallen as I heard audible smiles from several of the passengers.

But the remorseless railway man continued: "It is plain by the law of Canada that a passenger is not obliged to purchase a ticket before he enters the company's car; he may pay the conductor, if

[1] The Railway Act 1868, § 20.
[2] Jennings *v.* Gt. N. Rw., L. R., 1 Q. B. 7.
[3] Farewell *v.* G. T. R., 15 U. C. C. P. 427.

he pleases, the fare. But if the passenger pays and receives a ticket, then he accepts the ticket upon the condition that he will produce it and deliver it up when required by some duly authorized person, and in such case it is part of the contract:[1] so, my dear sir," he said soothingly to the gentleman, though to me his words were very swords, "please produce your ticket, or pay a second time. If you refuse, it will be too late for you to produce it when I have given the signal to stop the train to put you off."[2]

One lady, who appeared to be of the suspicious class, rather hesitated when the conductor requested her to give up her ticket, and take his check instead, but my friend told her that it was one of the rules of the line and that she was bound to obey it.[3]

When the conductor at length came up for my ticket I quietly shewed it, and telling him of the circumstances connected with the refusal of the baggage-man to check my trunk, asked him to refund the fare; this, as I expected, he refused to do, adding that my friend would do as a witness to prove that I had made the demand in case I chose to sue the company.

After this obnoxious individual had departed, the Q. C. entered into a lengthy disquisition concerning railway tickets; he remarked that the

1 Duke *v.* Great Western Rw., 14 U. C. Q. B. 377.
2 State *v.* Thompson, 20 N. H. 250.
3 N. R. Rw. *v.* Paige, 22 Barb. 130.

words usually printed on them, "'Good for this day only, A. to B.,' created a contract on the part of the company to convey the holder in one continuous journey from A. to B., to be commenced on the day of issuing the ticket, and that if a passenger alighted at an intermediate station he would forfeit all his rights under the ticket, and could not claim to be carried on to his journey's end in a subsequent train without paying a new fare.[1] And the same rule holds good when the ticket is marked "Good for this trip only;"[2] and when marked "Good for one passage on this day only," it can only be used on the day of its date.[3] And where a ticket with the words, "Good for this trip only," marked upon it, and unmutilated, but a few days old, was presented, it was held that it was *primâ facie* evidence that the holder had paid the regular fare, was entitled to be carried between the places named, and that the ticket had never been used; and also that such words referred to no particular trip, or time, but only to a continuous trip which might be made on the date or any subsequent day.[4] Some companies give their conductors power to allow passengers to

1 Briggs *v.* G. T. Rw., 24 U. C. Q. B., 510; Dietrich *v.* Penn. A. Rw., 8 C. L. J. (N. S.), 202; McClure *v.* Phil., Wil., & Balt. Rw., 34 Md. 532; Boice *v.* Hudson R. Rw., 61 Barb. 611; Cunningham *v.* G. T. R., 11 L. C. Jur. 107; Cheney *v.* Boston & M. Rw., 11 Met. 121; Elmore *v.* Sands, 54 N. Y. 512

2 Cheney *v.* Boston & Maine Rw., 11 Met. 121.

3 State *v.* Campbell, 3 Vroom, 309.

4 Pier *v.* Finch, 24 Barb. 514.

stop by the way by endorsing permission on the ticket.[1]

Companies have no intention of allowing a man after he has travelled on a ticket for a time by one train to leave it, and afterwards, at his august pleasure, to resume his seat in another train at some intervening part of the road ;[2] such proceedings would lead to endless confusion, trouble, and annoyance. But it appears that when one has tickets, in the coupon form, over distinct lines, if they contain no restrictions one may delay as long as he likes at the different changing places,[3] unless he voluntarily and negligently detaches the coupon.[4]

One Craig bought a ticket in Buffalo marked "Good only for twenty days from date," from Buffalo to Detroit. After viewing the glories and magnificence of thundering Niagara he took his seat in the afternoon accommodation train of the Great Western at the Suspension Bridge. This train ran on to London, but Craig for his own pleasure got out at St. Catherines and went up to see the town. As the night express was going through that fashionable watering-place he applied to be allowed to travel by it on the ticket he held, and on being refused sued the company. The court, however, considered that the ticket bound the company to carry the plaintiff on one contin-

[1] McClure *v.* Phil., Wil., & Balt. Rw., 34 Md. 532.

[2] State *v.* Overton, 4 Zabriskie, 438 ; Cincinnati, Columbus, & C. Rw. *v.* Bartram, 11 Ohio St. (U. S.), 457.

[3] Brooke *v.* Grand Trunk Rw , 15 Mich. 332

[4] Hamilton *v.* N. Y. C., 51 N. Y. 101.

uous journey from the Suspension Bridge to Detroit, giving him the option of taking any passenger train from the point of commencement, and if that train did not go the whole distance, to convey him the residue of the journey in some other train, the whole journey to be completed in twenty days; but that it did not give the holder the right to stop at every or any intermediate station as Mr. Craig contended.[1] If one has left the train in which he started on his journey, the fact that he has subsequently entered another train and travelled over a part of the remaining distance without being required to pay fare by the conductor in charge, does not prejudice the company or renew the contract.[2] But, said my friend, "I believe that in this last case Agnew, J., guarded his meaning by saying that there might be exceptions to the general rule, where from misfortune or accident, without his fault, the transit of the passenger is interrupted, and he afterwards resumes his journey. If, however, one has forfeited his right to be carried any further by his stopping over, and yet the company continue to carry him, they are bound to exercise reasonable care both towards him and towards his baggage.[3]

While I was listening intently to the words of knowledge that were flowing like some mighty river from the lips of the learned counsel, and

1 Craig v. Great Western Rw. Co., 24 U. C. Q. B. 504; Boston & Lowell Rw v. Proctor, 1 Allen, 267; Shedd v. Troy & Boston Rw., 40 Vt. 88.

2 Dietrich v. Penn. A. Rw. Co., 8 C. L. J. (N. S.), 202.

3 Smith v. G. T. R., 35 Q. B. (Ont.), 547, 557.

wondering how and why he was so deeply read on the topic, he suddenly stopped in his discourse, pointed his finger at a little child who had got possession of his mother's ticket and was quietly by a process of suction reducing it to an unsightly and undistinguishable pulp, then raising his voice, Smith, Q. C., exclaimed:—

"Excuse me, madam, you ought to be more careful of your ticket, for if you lose or destroy it, the conductor (unless he knows for a fact that you actually did pay your fare and obtain a ticket) will be justified in demanding repayment from you, and, if you refuse it, may put you off the cars. Just listen to what the late lamented Chief Justice Robinson says on this very point, and where a married woman, and for aught I know a mother like yourself, was turned off the train, or had to pay her fare a second time, I forget which."

And before the lady had recovered from her astonishment he dived into his red bag, produced an extensive brief, and reads as follows:—

"It may seem hard to a man who has lost his ticket, or perhaps had it stolen from him, that he should have to pay his fare a second time; but it is better and more reasonable that a passenger should now and then have to suffer the consequences of his own want of care, than that a system (the system of issuing tickets as now in vogue) should be rendered impracticable, which seems necessary to the transaction of this important branch of business. It is not for the sole advantage, or the pleasure and caprice of the railway company that these things are done in such a hurry. The public, whether wisely or not, desire to travel at the rate of four or five hundred miles a day, and that rapidity of movement cannot be accomplished without peculiar arrangements to suit the exigency which must be found sometimes to produce inconvenience. If the passenger in this case, who I have no doubt lost her ticket, could claim as a matter of right to have it believed on her word that she had paid her passage, everbody else in a similar case must have the same right to tell the same story and to be carried through without paying the conductor, and without showing to him a proof that he had paid any one."[1]

"But," said the lady, who during the delivery of the judgment had time to recover her senses and her ticket, "but my friend here could vouch for me that I spoke the truth."

"Ah, my dear madam, do not deceive yourself; reflect that in Massachusetts it was decided that if carriers require passengers to buy tickets before going on board, and to deliver them up on going off, and the passenger loses his ticket, he must on landing pay again;[2] and in Curtis *v.* G. T. R. Co.,[3] that ornament of the Canadian bench, Draper,

[1] Duke *v.* Great Western Rw. Co., 14 U. C. Q. B. 377.
[2] Standish *v.* Narragansett St. Co., 111 Mass. 512.
[3] 12 U. C. C. P. 89.

C. J., remarked that he supposed that a man who produced no ticket, but asserted that he had paid his fare and had lost his ticket and therefore declined to pay again, would — though a by-stander corroborated the assertion — be deemed refusing to pay, within the meaning of the Acts."

"I do not see what the Acts have to do with it. I never saw anything about such things in the Acts," said the lady, getting rather puzzled over the matter.

"What, madam, do you read such things? I should have imagined that a fair creature like yourself would have found them too dry to read."

"No sir; I am a member of the association of the Church of the New Jerusalem, and I read the Acts of the Apostles as well as every other part of the Bible," eagerly responded the lady.

Amid broad smiles, giggling he-hes, hearty ha-has, guffawing ho-hos, the Q. C. hastened to explain.

"Oh, my dear madam, I meant no allusion to Holy Writ; I meant 31 Vic., chapter 68, commonly called the Railway Act of 1868, which says at section 20: "Any passenger refusing to pay the fare, may by the conductor of the train and the servants the company be put off the cars, with his luggage, at any usual stopping-place, or near any dwelling-house, as the conductor elects, the conductor first stopping the train and using no unnecessary force."

CHAPTER IX.

PRODUCING TICKETS, OR EVICTION.

Carried past. — Jumping off. — Junctions. — Cave Canem. — Conductors refusing Change. — Fighting in the Cars. — Conduct of Passengers. — Ladies' Car. — Turned out in the Dark. — No Seats. — Colored Persons. — Tickets lost and found too late. — Conductor's Conduct. — Damages for Wrongful Ejectment. — Go quietly. — Companies heavily Mulcted. — By-law as to producing Tickets. — A Lover, his Mark. — Getting off for a Moment.

FORTUNATELY for my friend the attention of our fellow travellers was drawn away from him by the language, more forcible than elegant, of a man who had been carried past a small way-station at which he desired to alight, and for which he had a ticket. He vowed vengeance against the company because the train was not stopped and a reasonable opportunity given him to alight, and threatened loudly to sue the company for the damage which, he said, he would inevitably sustain through his non-delivery at his destination. And no doubt he would be successful, judging from authorities, in recovering compensation for the inconvenience, loss of time, and the labor of travelling back to the haven where he would be, because these are the direct consequences of the wrong done him.[1] One Hobbs, and Betsy his wife, with

[1] Damont *v.* N. O. & C. Rw., 9 Lou. Ann. 441; Ill. C. Rw. *v.* Able, 59 Ill. 131; Redfield on Railways, vol. ii., 276.

two juveniles, once took a midnight train homeward bound; they were landed, however, at another village, some miles off from their house; it was so late that they could neither get a conveyance, nor yet accommodation at an inn, and so all had to walk home through a drizzling rain. Betsy took cold and was laid up for some time, and the jury gave a verdict of £28 in their favor; £8 for the personal inconvenience, the balance for the wife's illness and its consequences. The court considered that Hobbs was entitled to the £8, but not to the rest, the sickness being too remote a consequence of the breach of contract.[1] This was in England, but in Mississippi where a man, subject to rheumatism, got carried past his station and had to walk back in the rain, whereupon his old enemy attacked him, it was decided that he might get satisfaction out of the company.[2] The ticket must always be taken to be the contract between the passenger and the company for the special purpose, and upon the terms which are contained in it,[3] and when the company has issued a ticket to a particular place they are bound to stop there, and it is not enough merely to slacken off steam;[4] but, without special agreement, one cannot insist upon a train stopping at a place where they do not usually delay."[5]

[1] Hobbs *v.* L. & S. W. Rw., L. R., 10 Q. B. 111.
[2] Mobile, etc., Rw. *v.* McArthur, 43 Miss. 180.
[3] Farewell *v.* G. T. R., 15 U. C. C. P. 427.
[4] Georgia Rw. *v.* McCurdy, 45 Ga. 288.
[5] Chicago, etc., Rw. *v.* Randolph, 53 Ill. 510

Somebody — not a Solomon — asked the man why he had not jumped off; he sensibly — considering he was in a passion — replied: —

"If I had been so foolhardy as to jump off while the train was in motion, without doubt, many a court in the land would hold that I did it at my own risk, and, if hurt, could coolly tell me that for my gross imprudence I had nobody but myself to blame,[1] if, however, they had stopped but for a moment, I would have run the risk of being injured by their starting before I was quite off, for then they would have been liable,[2] and I would have done so if the train had been moving slowly." [3]

"But," said my legal luminary to me, sotto-voce — for he was afraid to draw attention to himself again — "if a passenger is induced to leap from a car under the influence of a well-grounded fear of a collision that would be fatal to limb or life, it seems to be regarded as well settled that he may recover against the carriers, even though he would not have been hurt in the slightest degree, had he philosophically remained quiet." [4]

Another man wanted the conductor to stop the train because he had just discovered that he was on the wrong track; but this favor was refused,

[1] Damont *v.* N. O. & C. Rw. 9 Lou. Ann. 441; Lucas *v.* T. & N. B. Rw., 6 Gray, 64; but see Ill. C. Rw. *v.* Able, 59 Ill. 131.

[2] Penn. Rw. *v.* Kilgore, 32 Penn. St. 292.

[3] Filer *v.* N. Y. C., 49 N. Y. 47; Loyd *v.* Hannibal, etc., Rw., 53 Mo. 509.

[4] Ingalls *v.* Bills, 9 Met. 1; Eldridge *v.* Long Is. Rw, 1 Sandf. 89; Rw. *v* Aspell, 23 Penn. St. 147.

and the stupid fellow had to pay the full fare to the next stopping-place.[1]

By this time we had reached the Junction, and friend Smith and myself and several other persons got out to take the cars of the one or the other of the two other companies whose lines here cross. The stations of the three companies are all open to each other, and the passengers of each pass directly from the one to the other, "no pent up Utica contracts their powers" of pedestrianism, the whole area being used as common ground by the travellers on all three roads. While here, a porter of the B. and E. Co., who was trundling a track laden high with luggage, let a portmanteau fall off and injure the toes of one of our fellow-travellers who was on the part of the platform owned by the B. and E. Rw. Co. on his way to the terminus of the other line. (I afterwards heard that the court held that the negligence being an act of misfeasance by the servant of the company in the course of his employment, the maxim *respondeat superior* applied, and that the company were liable; but the judges doubted whether the railway would have been responsible supposing the man had been injured from the state and condition of the platform, as he had no business on it.)[2]

As I was trudging along an ugly dog of the cur

[1] Columbus, etc., Rw. *v.* Powell, 40 Ind. 37.

[2] Tebbutt *v.* Bristol & Ex. R. Co., L. R., 6 Q. B. 73; Stiles *v.* Cardiff Steam Nav. Co., 33 L. J. (N. S.), Q. B. 310

tribe, with a *noli me tangere* expression of countenance, dashed past me and rushed up to an innocent-looking individual, seizing him violently by the posterior part of the most indispensable portion of a man's attire, and judging from the row the fellow kicked up, by something more sensitive than pantaloons as well: shaking vigorously, the dog detached a piece of cloth and drew a little blood. The victim had a heavy stick in his hand, and the little doggy's lively career was stopped then and there. I remarked to the man, "My friend, if you find out that that unfortunate puppy belonged to the company or to any of their servants, sue them for damages; if not, don't trouble yourself to do so unless you can show that they were able to dispose of the fractious animal and did not do it."[1]

Shortly after we were again under way a little excitement was occasioned by an altercation between the conductor and a man who had not fully made up his mind (whether owing to the magnitude or insignificance thereof, we cannot say) how far he intended to ride, and so did not wish to settle for the present. The strife of tongues waxed warm, and the sound of the conflict rose high above the rattle and the din of the train.

The conductor said that if he did not at once pay the fare to some place or other he would have

[1] Smith *v.* Great Eastern Rw., L. R, 2 C. P. 4; Barrett *v.* Malden & Melrose Rw., 3 Allen, 101.

the pleasure of walking there. The man still hesitated, so the official pulled the check-rope, and on the stoppage of the train proceeded to eject the traveller, who at the last moment tendered a $20 gold piece, and told the conductor to take the fare to the next station (some $1.35). The latter declined now to receive the money, and put the man off, leaving him alone in his glory, breathing curses loud and deep.[1] Doubtless the official was justified in so doing, as in a somewhat similar case the court said that even an officer at a ticket office might reasonably object to an offer of a $20 gold piece to pay a fare of $1.35, on account of the trouble and risk involved: and that a person rushing into the cars without a ticket has no reason to expect that he will find the conductor prepared to change a $20 gold piece, for he relies upon receiving tickets from the passengers, or, if money be paid to him instead, he expects that it will be paid with reasonable regard to what is convenient under the circumstances.[2]

I may as well inform the general public here, that it is considered a reasonable condition for railway companies to require passengers to procure tickets before entering the train.[3]

My friend was just beginning to dilate upon the subject of ejecting passengers, when his voice was drowned by a crash, a scream, and a general up-

[1] People v. Jillson, 3 Parker C. C. 234.
[2] Fulton v. Grand Trunk Rw., 17 U. C. Q. B. 433.
[3] Hurst v. G. W. R., 19 C. B. (N. S.) 310.

rising of our fellow-travellers. I verily thought within myself that there was a collision — that we were off the track — that — that — that, I don't know what I did not think in the few moments that elapsed before I saw that it was only a fight between some men who had been indulging deeply in that cup which inebriates and brutalizes as well as cheers. The conductor soon arrived and quelled the disturbance. In this case, fortunately, it was not necessary — as it may sometimes be — for him to stop the train, call to his aid the engineer, the firemen, brakesmen and bellicose passengers, and leading the way himself — like some valiant knight of the Middle Ages — expel the disturbers of the peace, or else show by an earnest experiment that to do so was impossible.[1] If this latter contingency were to happen, the conductor must either discontinue the trip, or give the other passengers an opportunity of leaving the cars; otherwise the company will be responsible for the acts of the rioters.[2] A conductor is not bound to wait until some act of violence, profaneness, or other misconduct has been committed before exercising the power reposed in him of excluding or expelling offenders.[3] Of course he is never bound to receive passengers who will not conform to reasonable regulations, or who from their behavior, state of

[1] Pittsburgh, F. W., etc., Rw. *v.* Hinds, 7 Am. Reg. (N. S.) 14; *S. C.*, 53 Pa. St. 512.

[2] Redfield on Railways, vol. ii., p. 234.

[3] Vinton *v.* Middlesex Rw., 11 Allen, 306.

health or person, are offensive to the other travellers.[1]

Carriers of passengers are just as responsible for the misconduct of their living freight as they are for the mismanagement of the train. They must exercise the utmost vigilance in maintaining order — that first of Heaven's laws — and in guarding passengers against violence; or if not, they must pay for the consequences. In one case, they had to pay for the eye which a passenger lost, through the quarrel of some drunken men.[2] In another, for an arm broken in a shindy between votaries of Bacchus.[3] All disorderly and indecent conduct is to be repressed, and those sons of Belial who are guilty thereof must be excommunicated, or expelled, with Puritanic severity.[4] No one should be permitted to travel in a car, who so demeans himself as to endanger the safety, or interfere with the reasonable comfort and convenience of other passengers. But a wolf in sheep's clothing, a whited sepulchre, a serpent disguised as an angel of light, cannot be refused transport; nor need a conductor remove a too-far-gone dissenter from the principles of J. B. Gough, if he is neither disorderly nor offensive, nor if he remains quiet after admonition. If there is nothing in the condition, conduct, appearance, or manner of a passenger, from

1 Hodges on Railways, 553; 5th edit., 585.

2 Pittsburgh, etc., *v.* Pillow, 7 Leg. Gaz. 13; Sup. Ct Pa.

3 Pittsburgh, F. W., etc., Rw. *v.* Hinds, 7 Am. Reg. (N. S.) 14; *S. C.*, 53 Pa. St. 512.

4 Flint *v.* Norwich, etc., Transportation Co., 34 Conn. 554.

which it can reasonably be inferred that he means mischief, the company will not be liable for any sudden attack he may make upon another passenger.[1]

Where the company issue excursion tickets, stipulating to run trains in a particular manner, they cannot excuse themselves, by showing that the carriages are all filled.[2] In England, in ordinary cases, the ticket is issued subject to the condition that there is room in the train; otherwise those who are booked for the greatest distance have the preference.[3] And a carriage must not be suffered to become, or at least to continue overcrowded.[4] A considerable discussion has taken place in some of the States of the Republic as to how far railway companies can require colored persons to sit in a particular place or car. The right to do so was maintained by the Supreme Court of Pennsylvania,[5] but other tribunals have denied it. In Illinois it was decided that a company could not from caprice, wantonness, or prejudice, exclude a black woman from the ladies' car on account of her negro blood; although it might not be an unreasonable rule to require colored persons to occupy seats in a separate car, furnished as comfortably as the others.[6]

1 Putnam *v.* Broadway, etc., Rw., 55 N. Y. 108.
2 Patteson, J., in Hawcroft *v.* G. N. R., 16 Jur. 196.
3 Hodges on Railways, 553.
4 Jackson *v.* Metropolitan Rw., L. R., 10 C. P. 49.
5 Westchester Rw. *v.* Miles, 55 Penn. St. 209.
6 Chicago & N. W. *v.* Williams, 55 Ill. 185.

The duties of common carriers include the doing of everything calculated to render the transportation most comfortable and least annoying to passengers.[1] Their contract with their patrons is a stipulation for respectful treatment, that decency of demeanor which constitutes the charm of social life, that attention which mitigates evils without reluctance, and that promptitude which administers aid to distress. And in respect to women it proceeds still further; it includes an implied stipulation against general obscenity, that immodesty of approach which borders on lasciviousness, and against that wanton disregard of the feelings which aggravates every evil.[2]

As men of all sorts and conditions are so constantly travelling on trains, it is not only a reasonable regulation, but almost a humane duty, to have on every train a ladies' car for women and men accompanying them, from which creatures wearing exposed bifurcated garments, unblessed by the companionship of the fair sex, and women of offensive habits and character may be excluded, so that all the good ladies may be together as they will be in heaven.[3] And even though persons not admissible under the letter of the regulation are occasionally permitted within the charmed precincts the rule is still binding, and a male in trowsers has no right to enter without license or reason-

[1] Day *v.* Owen, 5 Mich. 520.
[2] Chamberlain *v.* Chandler, 3 Mason, 242; Nieto *v.* Clark, 1 Clifford, 145.
[3] Bass *v.* C. & N. W. Rw., 36 Wis. 450.

able excuse. If passengers excluded, by regulations, from the ladies' car cannot find seats in the regular coaches and there is room in the privileged place, they must not be kept standing; but it is the officers of the train who must determine who shall, or who shall not, be allowed to enter the presence of the ladies; one has no right to enter or attempt an entrance by force. If one being unable to find a seat elsewhere go peaceably into the ladies' car without being forbidden, he cannot then be removed by violence, unless a seat in another carriage is offered to him and he refuses to move. But under no circumstances will a brakesman be authorized in forcibly ejecting such an intruder by throwing him on to the platform while the train is crossing a river. A man is not bound to stay in a smoking-car.[1]

It is said to have been held by some court, in a case of *Toland* against *The Hudson River Railway*, that a passenger who is not provided with a seat is not obliged to pay any fare, and if expelled from the cars for refusing such payment may sustain an action against the company. But this doctrine must be taken *cum grano salis*. If a passenger is not accommodated as he should be, he may decline any compromise, and sue the company for refusing to carry him as their contract by the ticket or their duty required; and he doubtless will succeed unless the company prove

[1] Bass *v.* Chicago & N. W. Rw., 36 Wis. 450.

some just excuse. But if one chooses to accept a passage without a seat, the general understanding undoubtedly is that he must pay. If, however, he goes upon the cars expecting proper accommodation, and is put off because he declines going without, he may still sue.[1] So much by way of parenthesis and digression.

"Well, what have you got to say about ejectment?" I asked my chum.

"Oh, that it is deuced hard that every dunderhead of a conductor may put a poor wayfaring-man off, even at the noon of night, near any dwelling-house he may choose. In one case the night was dark and cloudy; from where the ejected man was placed, the lights of the last station were visible, although no house was nigh, yet the court held that the servants of the company had not exceeded their authority.[2] The law in some States is that one can only be put out at a station."[3]

"How would it be, old boy, if the poor wretch was short-sighted?" I inquired.

"That defect in one's optics would impose no additional obligation on the company; at least so it would appear from the authorities."[4]

"What would be the consequences if a fellow

[1] Redfield on Railways, vol. ii., p. 282; but see Davis *v.* Kansas City Rw., 58 Mo. 317.

[2] Fulton *v.* G. T. R., 17 U. C. Q. B. 433.

[3] Toledo, P., & W. Rw. *v.* Patterson, 63 Ill. 304.

[4] Bridges *v.* N. London Rw., L. R., 6 Q. B. 377.

was to mislay his ticket, and find it again after he had been ignominiously expelled; could he recover against the company?"

"I remember where one Curtis was travelling between St. Mary's and London, and had put his ticket away so safely — lest he should lose it — that he could not find it. The conductor called upon him to produce it; in vain Curtis ransacked pocket after pocket in coat, waistcoat, and trowsers, pulling out papers, letters, newspapers, wool, and all that precious olio to be found in a man's pockets. The other travellers were greatly edified and delighted at the exhibition of this *omnium gatherum*, and their laughs and jests added not a little to the confusion of the poor wretch searching for his little talismanic piece of pasteboard. At length the conductor stopped the train and turned C. off, though while being put off he offered to pay his fare. He sued the company, and got $300 out of them, the court holding the company liable for the acts of their officers duly authorized and styled (under the Act) conductors, when not committed in excess of authority, which in this case had not been overstepped. The company applied for a new trial, but the court declined to disturb the verdict (it being the second one recovered by Curtis), although it considered the damages excessive."[1]

"I should think," I remarked, "one ought to be allowed a reasonable time to find his ticket."

[1] Curtis v. G. T. R., 12 C. P. (U. C.), 89.

"Of course," was the reply, "a passenger has a right to ride so long as there is a reasonable expectation of his finding it during the trip.[1] A conductor on a previous train wrongfully taking the passenger's ticket does not excuse the traveller from producing it, when called upon by another conductor; although, in such a case, the company would be liable for the wrongful act of the first conductor."[2]

"I suppose the courts assume that the conductors are the agents of the company and authorized to do all legal acts for properly collecting the tickets, keeping order, running the train and removing persons who misbehave or will not pay, and such?" I queried.

"Yes," replied my friend, who was suffering from an acute attack of *cacoethes loquendi*, "and if in assuming to carry out what he is legally empowered to do, he forcibly removes from the cars (without any excuse) a passenger who has paid his fare, he will be liable for the assault; but if while being removed the man should slip, fall, and be injured, the company will not be responsible for his scratches and bruises, or his sprains and strains, such things being the remote, and not the proximate consequences of the ejectment."[3] Force may be used to prevent one un-

[1] Maples *v.* N. Y. & N. H. Rw., 38 Conn. 557.

[2] Townsend *v.* N. Y. C., 56 N. Y. 295; Hamilton *v.* N. Y. C., 51 N. Y. 100; but see Pittsburgh, etc., *v.* Hennigh, 39 Ind. 509; Palmer *v.* Charlotte, etc., Rw., 3 S. C. 580.

[3] Williamson *v.* G. T. R., 17 C. P. (U. C.), 615.

lawfully getting on a train and no liability be incurred for injuries; but when once a man is fairly on care must be taken in removing him.[1] Companies have a right to adopt such reasonable regulations as are necessary for their security, and if they are not complied with by the passengers, not only may the railroad refuse them admission to the cars, but if they are already within they may remove them;[2] and in the enforcement of order, and in the execution of reasonable regulations for the safety and comfort of passengers and for the security of the train, the authority of the officer in charge must be obeyed."[3]

"Suppose a man suffered serious detriment to his business by being wrongfully turned out of the cars, could he recover for such losses?" I asked.

"It has been so considered in the great Republic, if he declares specially in regard to them.[4] But it has been held — and I think rightly — that one cannot get vindictive or punitive damages against a company, unless they expressly or impliedly participate in the wrongful action by authorizing it beforehand or approving of it afterwards;[5] or the case be one of gross negligence or wilful misconduct."[6]

1 Kline *v.* Cent. Pac. Rw., 37 Cal. 400.

2 Stephen *v.* Smith, 29 Vt. 160.

3 Bass *v.* C. & N. W. Rw., 36 Wis. 463.

4 Holmes *v.* Doane, 3 Gray, 328.

5 Hagan *v.* Providence & W. Rw., 3 Rhode Island, 88.

6 Bannon *v.* Baltimore & O. R. R., 24 Md. 108; Baltimore & O. R. R. *v.* State, Ib. 271.

"What is it, then, exactly, that a man can get for being with indignity and insolence hustled out of a train, amid the laughs and jeers of the vulgar and the sneers of the polite?"

"Damages for actual injury, loss of time, pain of body, money paid to the doctor, or for injuries to the wounded feelings of the evicted one, may be allowed.[1] One man got $1,150 for being put off, when sick, away from a station."[2]

"Suppose one was killed, and sent off unprepared to the happy hunting grounds of his fathers?" I queried.

"Then the company would be liable under Lord Campbell's Act,"[3] answered my Nestor.

"I presume," I continued, still indulging my unquenchable thirst for knowledge, "that when a conductor gets into his cranium the idea that it is the proper thing to put one off, the best plan is quietly to submit to the inscrutable and go?"

"Undoubtedly — spoken like a veritable Solon. In such an evil case it will be wise and prudent to gather together one's surroundings and belongings, and peaceably succumb to the powers that be, for if you leave any articles behind you, you cannot recover their value, unless you can show that the company got them, or that the violence or suddenness of your ejection rendered it impossible for you to take them with you and so they

[1] Hagan v. Prov. & W. Rw., 3 Rhode Island, 88.
[2] Ill., etc., Rw. v. Sutton, 53 Ill. 397.
[3] Penn. Rw. Co. v. Vandiver, 42 Penn. St. 365.

were lost. This point Mr. Glover had the pleasure of settling. He was trying to do the London and Southwestern by giving half his ticket to a friend to save expenses, and when put out of the cars left a pair of glasses behind him, and the court told him that he had only himself to blame for the loss.[1] The courts never like the idea of mulcting railway companies in heavy damages for the sins of commission of their servants and conductors; and so where a verdict of £50 was given against the G. W. R. because the conductor put the plaintiff off the train, though the inconvenience to him was a mere bagatelle and the conductor had acted *bonâ fide* under an impression that the fare had not been paid, and had used no harshness or violence, a new trial was granted on the ground of excessive damages, and the Chief Justice stigmatized the verdict as 'outrageous:' but there the jurors of our Lady the Queen and my lord differed; and so on the second trial the yeomen of the county gave the man only £5 less, and the company submitted.[2] And in another case the same Canadian court spoke regretfully of the exorbitant amount of damages (£50) where the company were not otherwise concerned than through the act of their conductor, who thought that he had only been doing his duty, as England expects every man to do.[3] And where an Ameri-

[1] Glover *v.* London & S. W. Rw., 3 Q. B. 25.
[2] Huntsman *v.* G. W. R., 20 U. C. Q. B. 24.
[3] Davis *v.* G. W. R., 20 U. C. Q. B. 27, and Life of Lord Nelson.

can jury gave $1,000, no special damage being shown, a new trial was granted."[1]

"To return to the question of tickets." I said, "I saw an English decision the other day, which shows how one may save a little in going to an intermediate place, where opposition lines are running to some place beyond."

"How is that?" was asked.

"Why, often if two lines run to B. or there is an excursion thither, the fare is cheaper than to A., which, perhaps, is not half the distance, and one can buy a ticket to B. and get off at A. if he so wishes."

"Would that be a safe dodge?"

"It appears to have been decided in England that one may pay his fare to one place, and yet leave the cars at some intermediate place where the train stops, although the fare to the latter place may be greater than it is to the former."[2]

"I saw another rather funny decision. By a by-law, passengers not delivering up their tickets when required were made liable to a penalty; a man took a return ticket, yet after returning to the place whence he started, did not get off but went on to a further station, without, however, any intention to defraud; it was held that he could not be convicted under the by-law, for it only ap-

[1] Crocker *v.* New London, Will., & Pat. Rw., 24 Conn. 249.

[2] The Queen *v.* Frere, 4 E. & B. 598; Moore *v.* Metropolitan Rw., 8 Q. B. 36.

plied to the case of a person wilfully refusing to show his ticket *when he had one*, while here the man had none! It was held, also, that the by-law only applied to people travelling minus a ticket with intent to defraud.[1] Where a gentleman took tickets for himself and three servants, keeping the tickets in his own custody and telling the guard that he had them, and the servants were permitted to enter the car without having or showing each his ticket, the court held that the company were estopped from raising the objection that the by-law as to the production and delivery up of tickets had been infringed."[2]

"I believe," I remarked, when a pause enabled me to squeeze in a remark, "a company if it chooses may allow a discount off tickets bought before entering the cars; but that those who enter without their magic scraps of card-board cannot claim such indulgence,[3] even though they have been prevented purchasing them from the fact of the office being closed.[4] Although, I believe, it has been held by some courts that the increased rate cannot be collected unless every proper and reasonable facility has been afforded for procuring tickets at the station;[5] and that if a man, without

[1] Dearden *v.* Townsend, 12 Jur. (N. S.), 120; 35 L. J. Q. B. (N. S.), 98.
[2] Jennings *v.* G. N. R., 1 L. R. Q. B 7.
[3] The State *v.* Goold, 53 Maine, 279; Chicago and Alton Rw. *v.* Roberts, 40 Ill. 503.
[4] Crocker *v.* New London, Will., & Pat. Rw., 24 Conn. 249.
[5] St. Louis, etc., Rw. *v.* Dalby, 19 Ill. 353.

any default on his part, is prevented getting a ticket, he may pay the conductor the excess of fare under protest, and recover it back by suit, or else he may insist upon being taken at ticket rate, and sue for damages if the company refuse." [1]

"I see that in England some companies have a by-law that if a passenger loses his ticket he shall be liable to pay the full fare from the most distant place on the line."

"That 's rather hard lines."

"Don't pun — fortunately they cannot enforce their by-law by detaining the traveller himself." [2]

The legal disquisitions on railway companies were suffered to subside for a time, while the train rattled on. I gazed about on my companions. In the seat in front of me sat a young couple, and, judging from the orange blossoms in the bonnet of the one, and the clean shave and kid gloves of the other, not many hours had elapsed since they had stood side by side at Hymen's altar, and now they were seated inclining towards each other like the slanting sides of the letter A. The male had a little piece of sticking-plaster on his lower lip. As I was staring at the youthful couple, the train dashed into a tunnel and all was darkness. I heard a prolonged sucking sound as of a cow drawing her hind foot out of a mud-hole — to quote a western poet of renown — and when again we

[1] Jeffersonville, etc., Rw. *v.* Rogers, 28 Ind. 1.
[2] Chilton *v.* L. & C. Rw., 16 M. & W. 212.

emerged into the daylight, ho! presto! the plaster was reposing securely on the ruby lip of the orange-bonneted one; all else was serene and tranquil, and the two looked childlike and bland. How was this? here was a mystery as interesting as any involved in railway law. I meditated deeply on the point until I recollected what in our ante-nuptial days my Elizabeth and myself were wont to do; then all became clear and plain.

"Had a sleep, have you?" I said to my friend, who had been silent an hour and was now yawningly stretching himself.

"A sleep? oh! no! not even a cat-nap, scarcely worthy of the name of a kitten-nap," was the reply.

"Humph! rather a long kitten! twenty miles or so!"

We stopped at a small wayside station for a few minutes while the engine took a draught of water; a gentleman got out to take a breath of air or something of the sort, and while he was wandering up and down the platform, off started our train without a solitary premonitory screech, leaving the individual wildly waving his arms and frantically shouting after the hindermost car. In thus quietly slipping off, the company were wrong, for a traveller who alights temporarily, but without notice, invitation, or objection, while the train is stopping at an intermediate station, does no unlawful act, and although for a time he surrenders his place and rights as a passenger, he may resume them again before the train starts, and the officers of the railway are bound to give him reasonable notice of starting,[1] and must not steal off silently like a thief in the night. And passengers have a right to perambulate the platforms while the train is stopping for refreshments, and the firemen and stokers should not toss about wood or coal so as to injure the travellers.[2]

[1] State *v.* G. T. R., 4 Am. Rep. 258; 58 Me. 176.
[2] Jeffersonville, etc., Rw. *v.* Riley, 39 Ind. 568.

CHAPTER X.

PLATFORMS AND ALIGHTING.

Right to Safe Ingress, Egress, and Regress. — Defective Platforms. — The Englishman and the C'mum cat'or. — Getting out of Cars. — Train not at Platform. — Calling out Name; is it Invitation to alight? — Ladies jumping. — Hoop-skirts. — Must have Safe Place to alight. — Leaving Train in Motion.

"WELL, here we are at last at H.," said my friend who was learned in the law.

"Yes, now we have a chance of getting some grub (carefully collated from the plates of those who were here before us), and taking the epidermal covering off the interior of our mouths with a scalding decoction dignified by the name of tea," I replied.

"Ding-dong-all gone — come along — one-all," sounded forth the bell of the refreshment-room, as the train drew up to the platform, and all the weary travellers sprang up eager to stretch their limbs and to replenish the inner man. Out they rushed. Night had thrown her sable mantle (she has no other except for moonlight wear) over nature's tired bosom, so some of our fellow travellers, in the gloom, were precipitated into a hole in the platform, which the company carelessly suffered to be there — yawning open-mouthed — unmindful of the fact that passengers have the same rights to safe ingress, egress, regress, and progress over the stations and platforms at the intermediate places where the trains stop for refreshment, as they have at the termini of the line;[1] although it would appear that where a stoppage is made only for the purposes of the railway, and people are not expected to get in or out, the rights of the travelling public and the liability of the company are both greatly curtailed.[2] As soon as one procures a ticket he is to be regarded as a passenger, and is entitled to a safe passage to his seat.[3]

Though the unfortunates kissed mother earth, they were not seriously damaged; one indeed — as a medical witness afterwards put it — suffered "from a severe contusion of the integuments under the left orbit, with a great extravasation of blood and ecchymosis in the surrounding cellubas, having also a considerable abrasion of the cuticle," or, as the judge in common-place Anglo-Saxon expressed it, "had a black eye." Soon comestibles of all sorts, kinds, and descriptions were vanishing rapidly by means of down grades into sub-waistcoat and sub-bodice regions.

When we had finished our repast, the train still seemed quiescent, — appeared as motionless as a painted ship upon a painted ocean, — so it was

[1] McDonald *v.* Chicago, etc., 26 Iowa, 124.
[2] Frost *v.* Grand Trunk Rw., 10 Allen, 387.
[3] Warren *v.* Fitchburg Rw., 8 Allen, 227.

suggested that a little of something slightly stronger than tea might not be unpalatable; but, alas! spirits were tabooed on the line, so there was nothing for it but to make a foray into the adjoining neighborhood for additional stimulants. A porter kindly showed the way to a public house on the opposite side of the highroad passing the station. We were soon all practising with great success at the bar, but while enjoying ourselves to the full, the engine-bell rang out sharp and clear on the frosty air. Off we all rushed helter-skelter, and to save time, instead of returning by the way we came, we took what we thought was a bee-line for the station lights (but which turned out to be the engine's) across some unfenced ground. Before we well knew where we were we were all tumbling pell-mell, one over the other, into a wide ditch some three feet deep. However, we gained the cars in time, and then one of our chance acquaintances — who, having been leading in the race, went down first and was trampled upon by the rest — found that his arm was badly hurt; so the Q. C. and myself tried to console him with the assurance that he was safe to recover a verdict against the company if he only entrusted his case into the hands of either of us, for a railway company is bound so to fence its station that the public will not be misled, by seeing a place unfenced, into injuring themselves by passing that way, it being the shortest road to the platform.[1] (Though by the way, a Canadian court has considered that companies are not responsible if parties come to grief through taking short cuts, if the proper way of ingress and egress to the station is safe, convenient, and well-lighted;[2] but in another case a man who broke his leg in two places by falling into a culvert, constructed by the company in the highway, while leaving the station on a dark and stormy night, got $2,000 damages.)[3] The neglect properly to light a station, or to have a sufficient corps of servants to aid passengers in alighting at night, is evidence of negligence.[4]

Thinking that the man was an American citizen, I told him that Mr. C. J. Dillon, of the State of Iowa, had said on a comparatively recent occasion that "railway companies are bound to keep in a safe condition all portions of their platforms and approaches thereto to which the public do and would naturally resort, and all portions of their station-grounds reasonably near to the platforms, where passengers, or those who have purchased tickets with a view to take passage in their cars, would naturally or ordinarily be likely to go."[5]

"And, my dear sir," said the Q. C., who, more observant than myself, had noticed a pile of H's

[1] Burgess *v.* G. W. R., 32 L. J. 76.
[2] Walker *v.* G. W. R., 8 U. C. C. P. 161.
[3] Fairbanks *v.* G. W. R., 35 Q. B. (Ont.), 523.
[4] Patten *v.* Ch. & N. W. Rw., 36 Wis. 413.
[5] McDonald *v.* Chicago, etc., 26 Iowa, 124.

accumulating in front of the man, "there is a much stronger English case, where one Martin arrived at a station less than two minutes before the time for the train to leave, and while running along the line — in a place where he should not have gone — in order to reach the train which was a little ahead, he stumbled over a switch handle, fell on his elbow, and was considerably hurt. The jury considered that the company had been guilty of negligence and want of proper care, and gave Martin £20, and the court would not interfere."[1]

"Vell, hi think the Hinglish case is the one for my money," quoth our new found friend. "Hand hi'll rub my harm with a little hof this to prevent any 'arm," he added, producing a pocket comforter that Job never knew of.

"Don't waste good stuff that way," said Mr. Smith. "Apply it internally, and rub your arm with the bottle."

"Ho-ho-ho!" laughed John Bull at the wretched joke, which doubtless was first perpetrated "when the Memnonium was in all its glory." He took the advice, however, and the brandy with a vengeance.

Some little while after I saw him steadying himself as he stood up on the seat, and poking with his stick at the top of the car: supposing he was striving to open the ventilator, I paid little

[1] Martin *v.* Gt. Northern Rw., 16 C. B. 179; and see the case of stumbling over the hampers, Nicholson *v.* Lancashire & York Rw., 3 Hurl. & C. 534.

attention to him. In a few minutes the train suddenly stopped, — in a few seconds more the conductor came rushing into the car, excitedly asking if any one had pulled the rope or communicator.

"C'mum 'cat'or?" asked J. Bull, "I wang the bell for some bwandy 'n-vater. And dooced 'ard work hi 'ad to reach hit. Where 's the 'andle?"[1] Speedily the train was again under weigh.

At length, after several hours more of journeying we arrived at our destination, thankful that as yet all bones were safe and sound. Alas, I was hallooing before I was out of the wood, for as I emerged, the light being very dim, I fancied I was stepping on the platform, but as I landed violently on the ground I found that the car was some feet beyond the platform. Of course railways should bring their trains to a halt at places convenient for passengers to alight. Bringing a car to a solemn stand-still at a spot at which it is unsafe to get out, under circumstances which warrant one in believing that it is intended he shall alight and that he may do so in safety (without giving him warning of his danger), amounts to negligence on the part of the company, for which an action may be maintained if the passenger has not in any way contributed towards the accident.[2] This highly sensible rule

[1] See *Punch* for February, 1874.
[2] Cockle *v.* London & S. E. Rw. Co., L. R., 7 C. P. 721 (Ex. Ch.).

was adopted in the case of one Praeger, where — as I afterwards found — Lord Chief Justice Cockburn, of Geneva award renown, said: "I adopt most readily the formula which has been suggested as applicable to these cases, viz., that the company are bound to use reasonable care in providing accommodation for passengers, and that the passengers are also bound to use reasonable care in availing themselves of the accommodation provided for them."[1] Of course, if it had been daylight, and I could have used my eyesight to any practical purpose, and had noticed that the car was not in the ordinary position with regard to the platform, I would certainly have exercised a little more caution in getting out and not have been such a ninny-hammer as to step down in the way I did, for I can assure the general public, that it is anything but agreeable to step upon thin air and be thrown violently upon one's nasal organ, — which always seems tremendously projecting on such occasions, — abrasing one's elbows and knees.

As I had my homeward journey to perform by rail, and there seemed a chance of my being reduced to an atomic condition before I once again saw the wife of my bosom, I then, for the benefit of my numerous readers (for, of course, I meant to publish a book, as every one does nowadays), dotted down a few decisions which I thought might

[1] Praeger *v.* Bristol & Exeter Rw., 24 L. T. (N. S.) 105.

be useful for them to bear in mind in case they ever came to grief in alighting from a railway train ; and here they are *pro bono publico.*

(N. B. — Those frivolous persons who only read to pass the time, had better turn at once to the next chapter.)

Where the train overshot the platform so that the car in which one Whitaker was sitting stood opposite to the parapet of a bridge, the top of which in the dusk looked like the platform ; the porters having called out the name of the place, W. getting out on the parapet in the *bonâ fide* belief that he was stepping on the platform, fell over and was injured, but recovered from the company. Bovill, C. J., held that on this occasion there was a clear invitation to alight at a dangerous place, and that W. was misled by the appearance of the parapet, and so distinguished the case from the Bridges one, to which I will refer in a moment or two.[1] Where in the dark, a passenger on alighting fell into a culvert, over which the car had stopped, the company were held liable.[2]

Owing to the length of the train in which a Mr. and Mrs. Foy were journeying, there was not room for all the cars to be drawn up at the platform, and some of the passengers were desired to get out upon the line beyond it. The distance from the carriage to the ground was only three

[1] Whitaker v. Manchester & S. Rw. Co., L. R., 5 C. P. 464.
[2] Col. & Ind. C. Rw. Co. v. Farrell, 31 Ind. 408.

feet; Mrs. F. (instead of sensibly availing herself of the two steps of the carriage) with the aid of Mr. Foy jumped from the first step to the ground, and — not being a practised athlete or gymnast but a sweet little thing — came down upon the ground like a barrel of sugar with such a thud that the vertebræ of her back were jarred and the spine injured. The jury found that the company were guilty of negligence in not providing reasonable means of alighting, and that the lady had not contributed to the accident, and they gave her £500 to pay her doctor's bills; and the court considered the verdict warranted and declined to interfere with the damages.[1] Bovill, Q. C., urged that if the lady, instead of jumping as she did, had turned herself round and availed herself of the assistance of both steps and of the handles of the carriage, the accident would not have happened; but Williams, J., said severely that "in the present fashion of female attire, the mode of descent suggested by the learned counsel would be scarcely decent!" This judgment was given in 1865, and as fashions change two or three times a year, one can hardly decide what a lady might or should do in this present year of grace, especially as the virtuous judge did not insinuate wherein in such a descent would lie the lack of woman's crowning glory, modesty.

While speaking of ladies and their attire I may

[3] Foy & Wife v. London, B., & S. C. Rw. Co., 18 C. B. (N. S.), 225.

mention that Mrs. Mary Poulin, while alighting from a Broadway car, with her youngest hopeful in her arms, caught her steel hoop-skirt upon a nail in the car platform ; this threw her down, and she was dragged some distance, and seriously injured and greatly frightened. The company tried to escape liability by the ungallant plea that hoops were not a necessary article of female apparel and that if Mrs. P. was determined to wear such inflated skirts she ought to have exercised more care than is required of a brother in sit-upons ; the court, however, differed from the company, and considered that the fair lady had been guilty of no negligence, and that if the railroad carried passengers adorned with crinolines they must see to their safety.[1]

Old Siner and his wife arrived in daylight at Rhyl Station and the carriage in which they were overshot the platform ; the passengers were neither told to keep their seats nor to get out, nor did the train move until it started on its forward journey. After exhausting his stock of patience, S. following the example of his fellow travellers alighted, without asking the company's servants to back the train to the platform or holding any communication with them whatever. The wife then, standing on the iron steps of the carriage, grasped both her husband's hands and jumped down, straining her knee in the act. She did not use the foot-

[1] Poulin v. Broadway, etc., Rw., 34 N. Y. Sup. Ct. 296.

board. There was no evidence of any carelessness or awkwardness except what might be inferred from these facts. In an action brought against the company for this injury, the court held (Kelly, C. B. *diss.*) that there was no evidence of negligence in the defendants, and that the accident was entirely the result of the woman's own act in awkwardly and carelessly jumping.[1] The *Foy* case was distinguished, as there an express invitation to alight was given.

Where a gentleman, the corneas of whose eyes were far more convex than those of the generality of the genus *homo*, knowing well the station, got out of the train while the carriage in which he had been sitting was still in a tunnel, and in making his way to the platform stumbled over some rubbish and fell, breaking his leg and otherwise injuring himself so that he shortly died from the effects, it was held by the House of Lords (reversing the decision of the court below) that the train having come to a stand-still, the calling out the name of the place was an invitation to alight, and that the company's servants calling out afterwards " Keep your seats," showed that it had been improvidently uttered, and therefore furnished evidence of negligence, and that the personal representative of Mr. Bridges was entitled to recover against the company.[2] The shortsightedness of

[1] Siner *v.* G. W. R., L. R., 3 Ex. 150.

[2] Bridges *v.* North London Rw. Co., L. R., 6 Q. B. 377. In appeal L. R., 7 H. L. 213.

the deceased imposed no additional duties on the company. In another case the court thought that the conduct of a traveller, who fell down between the car and the platform, which curved gracefully back from the line, amounted to contributory negligence and so made absolute a rule to enter a nonsuit.[1]

In Bridges' case it was unanimously held by the whole court, that the calling out the name of a station is not in itself an intimation to the passengers to alight; whether it is so or not must depend on the circumstances of each particular case. Willes, J., said, "Nobody who travels by rail who has a head on his shoulders would ever say that calling out the name was an invitation;" but many a man with a head on his shoulders, and with something in that head too, acts as if he did, — indeed C. J. Redfield says that Bridges only did what the great majority of men would have done under similar circumstances. (In fact Redfield considers that in the late cases the English courts have overstrained things in favor of the companies.)[2] Baron Cleasby thought that in reality the stopping of the train at the station is the invitation to alight. Bovill, C. J., said that whether calling out was a request to get out or not was a question for a jury.[3] In a late case

[1] Praeger *v.* Bristol & Exeter Rw., L. R., 5 C. P. 460, n. 1; also Plant *v.* Midland Rw. Co., 21 L. T. (N. S.), 836; and Harrold *v.* Great Western Rw., 14 L. T. (N. S.), 440.

[2] Redfield on Railways, vol. ii., p. 264.

[3] Whitaker *v.* Manchester & S. Rw., L. R., 5 C. P. 464.

Mr. Justice Blackburn gave it as his decided opinion, that calling out the name is merely an intimation to all on the train that the place at which the cars are about to stop is that particular station named; and he adds (most truthfully) that every person must have heard porters at stations call out something which, if the traveller happens to know the name of the place, is recognizable, but if the name is not known, no reliable information is gained from the porter's cry.[1] In a still later case it was said that the train having overshot the platform and the name of the place having been called out, the omission of the company's servants to caution passengers not to alight until the train had been brought up at the proper place was evidence of negligence, or according to Honeyman, J., negligence itself.[2]

Companies are bound to provide platforms, or safe places of deposit, for passengers to alight on at their stations and to deliver them there. If there is any difficulty in the passengers' getting out, the officers should assist them to do so.[3] If the place where one is required to alight is in fact dangerous, it is his duty to request the train to be put in its proper place; and this is a request which no station-master would venture to refuse, knowing

[1] Lewis & Wife v. London C. & D. Rw., L. R., 9 Q. B. 69; Cockle v. London & S. E. Rw., L. R., 5 C. P. 457 (Ex. Ch.), distinguished.

[2] Weller v. London, Brighton, & S. C. Rw., L. R., 9 C. P. 126.

[3] Memphis & Charleston Rw. v. Whitfield, 44 Miss. 466; Robson v. N. E. Rw., L. R., 10 Q. B. 271.

the risk he would incur if an accident happened through his refusal. If the defendants will not place the train properly, the plaintiff should stay in the carriage. So, at least, said the judges in Siner *v.* Great Western Railway (*supra*);[1] but we can well imagine the surprised look — tinged strongly with scorn — of a conductor upon any one of our Cis-atlantic railways, were he asked to move his train forwards or backwards merely for the convenience of his living freight.

If a man persists in getting off a train while it is in motion, especially if he has been warned by the conductor not to do so, he has no claim against the company for any damage he may receive in the act;[2] and so when one attemped to get on a train while moving and was killed in the attempt, it was held, as a matter of law, that no recovery could be had.[3] But otherwise where one lost his life in jumping off by the direction of the conductor.[4] The courts of Mississippi have laid it down clearly that it is the duty of railway companies to announce audibly in each car the name of the station reached and then allow sufficient time for the passengers safely to leave the carriages; and that on the other hand it is the duty of the passengers to use reasonable care, and to conform to the customs and usages of the company so far as

1 See also, Memphis & C. Rw. *v.* Whitfield, 44 Miss. 466.

2 Ohio & Miss. Rw. *v.* Schiebe, 44 Ill. 460.

3 Knight *v.* Ponchartrain Rw., 23 La. Ann. 462.

4 Lambeth *v.* North Carolina Rw., 66 N. C. 494.

they know and understand them.[1] If a company through neglect of their duty expose a passenger to obvious peril, or grave inconvenience, and the traveller to escape the threatened peril, or inconvenience, does something that is not obviously dangerous (although it may be the cause of the injury) the company will be liable.[2]

Where a man is so drunk that he cannot take care of himself, if the conductor is aware of it, he must bestow upon him the requisite degree of attention to save him from injury; [3] and so when a traveller is sick.

Ah me! I fear that this long dilating will cause my Diary to be sent

> To bind a book, to line a box,
> Or serve to curl a maiden's locks.

[1] Southern Rw. *v.* Kendrick, 40 Miss. 374.
[2] Adams *v.* Lancashire & Y. Rw., L. R., 4 C. P. 744.
[3] Giles *v.* G. W. R., 36 Q. B. (Ont.) 360.

CHAPTER XI.

BAGGAGE.

Gone. — Company liable for Lost Baggage. — Carelessness of Owner. — Checking. — What is Baggage? — Papers. — Spring-horse. — Household Goods going West. — Luggage left in Cloak-room. — Limitation of Liability. — Taking Change. — Railroad Police. — Beauties of Checks. — Fall of a Window. — Legs and Arms outside. — Officials squeezing Fingers. — Stern Boreas.

MISFORTUNES never come singly, for birds of a feather flock together. Scarcely had I got to the hotel and begun ruefully examining the discolorations on my nether limbs and putting a piece of sticking-plaster on the top of my proboscis, when a thought struck me, and really hurt me, so that I involuntarily exclaimed, "Why, where 's my bag?" Of one thing I was soon satisfied, namely, that it was not there. I ran my fingers through my hair to let the cooling air as near as possible to my heated brain, and after mature reflection came to the conclusion that I had seen nothing of it since I had left it in the car while I went out after those refreshments already referred to; for on my return, finding in my seat a lovely girl, with long dark eyelashes, soft tender dark-blue eyes, a bewitching smile, and dimples which rippled round her ruby lips as she talked and laughed with a young fellow of a vinegar aspect who sat beside her, I had located myself elsewhere. Both these individuals had got out at the next station, but I had never again noticed, or even thought of, my bag.

When I met the Q. C. in the dining-hall I told him of my loss.

"What had you in your bag?" he inquired, with the air of a man who thought that he knew a thing or two about lost luggage.

"Nothing but my brushes and razors, pen and ink; some shirt-fronts *alias* dickeys, and other clothing."

"Ah well! you are all right! you can easily recover the value of the waifs and strays from the company; for all those things have been held to be such personal baggage as a traveller has a right to carry with him.[1] Have you got your check?" he added.

"No. It was not checked. I carried it into the car with me, and left it to keep my place when we got out for refreshments, and it was gone before I got back into my seat — at least I have not beheld it since."

"*N'importe!* as the frog-eaters say. You are entitled to recover, for your ticket gives you a right to be carried with your luggage;[2] and a by-

[1] Hawkins *v.* Hoffman, 6 Hill (N. Y.), 586; Duffy *v.* Thompson, 4 E. D. Smith, 178.

[2] Gamble *v.* G. W. Rw., 24 U. C. Q. B. 407; Le Conteur *v.* London & S. W. Rw., L. R., 1 Q. B. 54.

law to the effect that a company will not be responsible for baggage unless booked, has been held bad in England.[1] Of course, if you had kept exclusive control over your bag, the company would not ordinarily be liable.[2] And when a man has his traps taken into the car with him for his own convenience he impliedly undertakes to use reasonable care; and if one were to leave his portmanteau in one car while he went and travelled in another, and the portmanteau was rifled, he could not recover for his loss;[3] nor, if he stupidly forgot to take his overcoat with him, when he left the train."[4]

"I had an idea," I said, "that a Canadian judge had expressed an opinion to the effect that the system of checking in vogue in this enlightened country was notice to passengers that all articles must be checked or handed to the company's servants, except what they desire or prefer to keep under their own personal care and at their own risk. Did you ever meet with such a dictum or decision?"

"Oh yes, I noticed the case only the other day. Morrison, J., did speak to that effect, but he was overruled, and Draper, C. J., said that he considered checking only as additional precautions

[1] Williams *v.* G. W. Rw., 10 Ex. 15; see also, G. W. R. *v.* Goodman, 12 C. B. 313.

[2] Tower *v.* Utica & Sch. Rw., 7 Hill (N. Y.), 47; and Wilde, J., in Richards *v.* London, B., & S. C. Rw., 7 C. B. 839.

[3] Talley *v.* G. W. R., L. R., 6 C. P. 44.

[4] Tower *v.* Utica & Sch. Rw., *supra*

taken by the company, beyond what is customary in England, in order to prevent the luggage from being given up to the wrong person; that the company would be liable for a loss in case no such means of checking was in use, and if, notwithstanding, a loss occurs, the liability is unchanged, in the absence of express notice on their part that they will be responsible only for articles checked.[1] By the way, were there any papers in your bag?"

"No; they were all in my pocket. I have not many with me, and I remember seeing it decided that title deeds, which an attorney was carrying with him to produce on a trial, were not baggage for the loss of which a carrier would be responsible."[2]

"Prudent man!" replied my friend, as he turned on his heel and departed.

What I did at the place where I now was concerns nobody except those who had the pleasure of paying my travelling expenses to and fro and my hotel bill while there. To dilate with any particularity on the subject might lead one into a breach of that well-established rule concerning privileged communications between attorneys and their clients.

At length my labors were at an end and I was at perfect liberty to return to my *Lares et Penates* at my earliest convenience. My readers must not suppose, from the fact that my bag and baggage

[1] Gamble *v.* Great Western Rw., 24 U. C. Q. B. 407.
[2] Phelps *v.* London & N. W. Rw., 19 C. B. (N. S.), 321.

had been lost, that I was acting the Nazarite all this time; no indeed, I had bought all the necessary articles of a gentleman's toilet and some changes of raiment, and with these in a bran new valise I was ready to start *en route* for the place whence I had come forth.

I was rather amused, while awaiting the arrival of my train at the station, by a controversy between what was evidently a "fond parient" of rural origin and the baggage-master. The father had invested in a spring-horse for his youthful son and heir to exercise upon; the creature was forty-four inches long and weighed seventy-eight pounds. The man wished it passed as luggage.

"No, you will have to pay freight for this," said he of the chalk and checks.

"But I have nothing else, and I am certainly entitled to carry something," urged the man.

"Yes," returned the other, "you are entitled to take your personal baggage with you; but if you have none, that does not give you the right to take other things instead,[1] and a horse of this color is personal luggage by no manner of means." [2]

Just then a friend came up to me and asked what was included in the personal baggage which a man was entitled to take with him, free of charge. I said: —

1 Pardee *v.* Drew, 25 Wend. 459.
2 Hudston *v.* Midland Rw., L. R., 4 Q. B. 366.

"My dear sir, that is a question which has often pressed itself seriously upon the consideration of a contemplative traveller and philosophic jurist like myself, when on entering a crowded train I have found one half of the seats occupied by 'stern realities' or bipedal extremities, and the other half by bundles and bandboxes, nursery paraphernalia, and the oleaginous and saccharine products of the kitchen and the cook-shop ; and also when I have considered how gravely the question has agitated courts of justice. One of our own learned judges has forcibly remarked that 'the authorities and references show it is much easier to say what is not personal or ordinary luggage, than it is to decide what it is which a carrier is bound, or which it is usual for him to carry along with his passengers.'"

"You have made a long oration, but have not answered my question; just like you lawyers, always darkening counsel by words."

"State your question more definitely," I remarked.

"Well, then, there is a poor man here, moving West with his family. He has a bed, pillows, bolsters, and bed-quilt in a trunk, or a box, with his clothes; he is carrying them for his own use. Should he be compelled to pay freight on them? He says that he has no money; and I don't want to see the poor beggar put upon."

"Yours is a question which I cannot definitely

answer. In England, it was decided that such things were not personal baggage.[1] In Vermont it was held a matter for a jury to pronounce upon, after considering the peculiar circumstances, the value, the quantity, and the intended use of the articles."[2]

" 'He would not, with a peremptory tone,
Assert the nose upon his face, his own;
With hesitation, admirably slow,
He humbly hopes, presumes it may be so.' "

said my friend mockingly, and then added pepperishly, "You unsatisfactory lawyers will never give a sensible reply to the simplest question."

"Granted. But yours was not the simplest question. Were an ordinary layman like yourself to read but a tithe of what has been written on the moot point of personal luggage or not, you would be a sadder, if not a wiser man than you now are; so voluminous are the decisions, that a Saratoga trunk would fail to contain all."

"Well, you are not luminous anyway.

" 'Lawyers each dark question shun
And hold their farthing candle to the sun.'

I 'm off to get my traps in the cloak-room."

"I 'll go with you," I replied.

When we got to the room we found the door locked, and that the man in charge was off for an hour or so.

"Well, that is a pretty how-do-ye-do; my train

[1] Macrow *v.* Gt. Western Rw. Co., L. R., 6 Q. B. 612.
[2] Ouimit *v.* Henshaw, 35 Vt. 605.

will be going in a few minutes, so what am I to do?"

"Have you got a ticket for your baggage?" I inquired.

"Yes, and paid tuppence for it. Here it is." On the back of it were some printed conditions, but nothing was said as to the hours the cloak-room was kept open, or at what time the box was to be re-delivered.

"It is clear," I remarked, "that the company is bound to give you your box on your reasonable request, and at any reasonable time."[1]

"But what good does that do me, if they are not here to give me my things now? I must go on whether I get them or not."

"You can sue them," I remarked.

"All very fine, but I have a case of patterns which I need with me; and suppose it is lost?"

"Well, of course, you can't recover damages beyond the actual value of the goods. No warehouseman is responsible beyond the actual value of the article lost or damaged, unless there was a special contract.[2] What was the value?"

"Thirty or forty pounds."

"What!"

"Can't you hear? I say thirty or forty pounds."

"Well, I am very sorry for you. Did not you see the notice on the ticket that 'the company

[1] Stallard v. Gt. W. R., 2 B. & S. 419; 8 Jur. (N. S.), 1076.

[2] Anderson v. Northeastern Rw., 4 L. T. (N. S.), 216.

will not be responsible for any package exceeding the value of £10.' "

"Oh, but I did not read that."

"The legal inference, however, is that you did read it, and did assent to it; and so I am afraid that the company, in case of a loss, will not be liable as your goods exceed the prescribed limit.[1] For the same reason they may also be excused for delay in redelivering them, at least if such tardiness is not caused by any wilful act or default of their own, and is without their privity or knowledge.[2] Samples and patterns are not considered personal baggage." [3]

"Many thanks for all your information. I think I can see my box through this crack, and here comes the man with the key; so I am all right."

"Well, good-by! there 's my train, anyway, so I am off. Don't forget you owe me a fee for this."

As I was passing into the car, I saw a crowd gathered round the ticket-office, and an unfortunate man — quite respectably habited — struggling in the clutches of a policeman. I made inquiries as to the cause of the arrest and was told that the prisoner had been buying a ticket at the office, and in giving change the clerk handed him two sous, a French piece; the man, whose name

[1] Van Toll *v.* Southeastern Rw. Co., 12 C. B. (N. S.), 75; 6 L. T. (N. S.), 244; Harris *v.* G. W. R., W. N. June 10, 1876; but see Henderson *v.* Stevenson, L R., 2 S. & D. 470.

[2] Pepper *v.* Southeastern Rw. Co., 17 L. T. (N. S.), 469.

[3] Bayley *v.* Lancaster Rw. Co., 18 Sol. J. 301.

was Allen, objected and demanded a British penny in its place, and as the clerk would not take back the sous, Allen determined to help himself. The bowl of the till containing copper coins appearing to be within easy reach he put in his hand to get the money. Upon this the agent raised the hue and cry, summoned the conservator of the peace on duty and gave A. into custody on the charge of attempting to rob the till. It seemed rather a hard case, as the poor fellow was only trying to help himself to his change. (Being dubious as to what would be the upshot of the affair I bore the matter in mind, and after the usual time required for issuing a writ, bringing a case to trial, moving in term and giving judgment, I discovered that in the action brought by A. against the company for false imprisonment it was held, that as the arrest, after the attempt had ceased, could not be necessary for the protection of the company's property, but was merely to vindicate justice, the clerk had no implied authority to arrest the man; his authority only extended to the doing of such acts as were necessary for the fulfillment of the duties entrusted to him, and that the company was, therefore, not liable for the act of the clerk, nor for that of the policeman who took A. into custody. Blackburn, J., was inclined to think that if a man in charge of a till were to find that a person was attempting to rob it, and he could only prevent his stealing by taking him into custody, he might have an implied authority to arrest the offender; or, if the clerk had reason to believe that the money had been actually stolen and he could get it back by taking the thief into custody, and he took him up for that purpose, it might be that that also would be within the authority of the clerk.[1])

A man standing by me asked how it was that the policeman had not on the same style of garments as those of his fellows who perambulate in blissful ease and quiet serenity the city streets. I told him that railway companies had power to appoint constables to act on their lines for the preservation of peace, and securing persons and property against felonies and other unlawful acts on such railways and their works, and in all places not more than a quarter of a mile distant therefrom, and to take before a justice of the peace any person guilty of an offence punishable by summary convictions under any act or by-law.[2]

This time I had my *impedimenta* checked, and thus was relieved of the trouble of carrying them in and out of the car. All the world knows that the possession of a check is evidence against the company of the receipt of the baggage. The piece of metal has been compared to a bill of lading, in fact said to be identical therewith.[3] It is always the source of great wonderment to me that the British public do not insist upon the British rail-

[1] Allen *v.* London & S. W. Rw., L. R., 6 Q. B. 65.
[2] Railway Act, 1868, § 49.
[3] Dill *v.* Railroad Co., 7 Rich 158.

ways introducing the system on their lines; the continental plan of registering, though far in advance of the English, is still much more troublesome than the simple process of checking, and very expensive. How convenient is our enlightened plan, when one has to change cars *en route :* no trouble looking after baggage ; one simply has to walk out of one train into the other, ticket for the whole journey and checks in your pocket, and if your traps are lost, you can sue either or any of the companies.[1]

The car being rather crowded, the atmosphere soon became rather close and stifling. A gentleman, after a considerable amount of coaxing, pushing, shoving, and pulling, persuaded one of the windows to allow itself to be lifted up to admit the sharp, clear, exhilarating winter's air. The person who opened the window got out and another got in and took his seat beside it, and carelessly allowed his left hand to rest on the ledge. As the train approached a station, the breaks were suddenly put on, and the vibration caused the window to fall athwart the man's fingers, inflicting a serious injury thereon. Aroused and attracted by the grunting and groaning, adjurations and exclamations of the injured one, some officious people came round him, advising and urging the poor fellow to sue the company, for that they were bound to provide windows with good fastenings for the comfort

[1] Hart *v.* Rensellaer & Saratoga Rw., 4 Seld. 37.

and protection of passengers. I merely said, that without positive proof of the defective construction of the window, the mere falling would not make a *primâ facie* case of negligence against the company, as a Mr. Murray found when he sued a London railway company for exactly a similar injury.[1]

Some people seem to be possessed of limbs which do not appear to belong to them of right, and with which they never seem to know exactly what to do; and such uncomfortably constituted mortals are very apt to stretch their heads, or legs, or arms, out of the windows of railway carriages, having no other improper place to put them when travelling by rail; to such eccentric genii I would remark, that if they are injured while in this position, they will not be able to recover damages against the company, for the negligence is their own, and the company is not bound to put bars across its carriage windows as careful matrons do over their nursery panes.[2] It was once held that a company, in order to save the upper extremities of their passengers, was bound to provide wire gauzes, bars, slats, or other barricades for the windows,[3] but this fatherly decision has been overruled.[4] Mrs. Holbrook found this to her cost

1 Murray *v.* Metropolitan District Rw., 27 L. T. (N. S.), 762.

2 Indianapolis & Cincinnati Rw. *v.* Rutherford, 7 Am. Law Reg. (N. S.), 476.

3 N. J. R. *v.* Kennard, 21 Penn. St., 203.

4 P. & C. Rw. *v.* McClurg, 7 Am. Law Reg. (N. S.), 277; Pittsburgh, etc., Rw. *v.* Andrews, 39 Md. 329.

when she had her arm broken (it was projecting from the window) by something coming against it as they were passing other cars on another track.[1] In the State where the principles of brotherly love prevail, or are supposed to, it was held that when passengers are liable to have their arms, if lying outside the windows, caught in passing bridges, the conductors should give them notice to put them effectually upon their guard, or the company will be liable for injuries, and printed notices are not sufficient.[2]

Talking about squeezing fingers — a decidedly unpleasant thing to the squeezee, when not done by the human hand divine — railway officials are not allowed, as a rule, to apply extempore thumbscrews and pinch a man's digits in the door. This has been solemnly decided by the Court of Common Pleas, at Westminster Hall. One Fordham was in the act of getting into a railway carriage, of the usual English make with doors at the sides opening outwards; having a parcel in his right hand, he very naturally placed his left on the open door to aid him on entering. The guard, without giving any previous warning, flung to the door with a slam. F. having just at that moment his fingers where the door should meet the door-plate, and they possessing that quality of matter, compressibility, he had them

[1] Holbrook *v.* Utica & Sch. Rw., 12 N. Y. 236.
[2] Laing *v.* Colder, 8 Penn. St. 483.

badly crushed. The Court of Common Pleas and the Exchequer Chamber thought that the guard had been guilty of carelessness, and that Fordham had done nothing to contribute thereto, and so gave the latter damages against the railway company.[1] Mr. Jackson made £50 out of his ride from Moorgate Street to Westbourne Park by the underground railroad. The compartment in which he was seated was full, but at Gower Street two more got in despite our friend's remonstrances. At the next station others tried to enter (the door having been opened), but were prevented by those in possession. The door remained unshut as the train passed along the platform, but just as it entered the tunnel the porter slammed it to, and jammed Jackson's hand in the hinge. The court considered that all these facts showed such a careless and improper mode of conducting business that Jackson was entitled to keep the little sum mentioned.[2]

In another case, however, where a porter after he had called out, " Take your seats — take your seats ! " squeezed a man's thumb in shutting to the door, the same court considered that the official had closed the door in the ordinary and proper exercise of his duty, and that Mr. Richardson had only to thank himself for his want of caution in leav-

[1] Fordham *v.* L. B. & S. C. Rw., L. R., 3 C. P. 368 ; 4 C. P. 619 (Ex. Ch.); also, Coleman *v.* S. E. Rw., 4 H. & C. 699.

[2] Jackson *v.* Metropolitan Rw., L. R., 10 C. P. 49.

ing his member where it might be so easily crushed.[1]

To return from this digression, which my readers will probably have found as dull and heavy as most wanderings of that nature. Before many hours had passed, thick heavy clouds began to scud across the sky; the wind sighed and moaned mournfully around the car; Boreas came raging from the icy regions of the North, and the snowflakes whirled wildly in ever-thickening clouds — as a Longfellow would have said had he been on board that express train: —

Ever thicker, thicker, thicker,
Froze the ice on lake and river:
Ever deeper, deeper, deeper,
Fell the snow o'er all the landscape,
Fell the covering snow and drifted
Through the forest, round the carriage.

Slowly and more slowly did the laboring engine, laden with its long line of cars, make its way against the obstructing showers of feathery ice-morsels, and fears arose in the hearts of the passengers that our progress would soon be entirely stopped and we would be left to spend the long cold night imbedded in the rapidly rising banks of snow.

A lady, shivering as she gazed out into the now pitchy darkness, asked me in quivering tones, what would be done if we came to a complete standstill and the engine was unable to move at all? I replied: —

[1] Richardson v. Metropolitan Rw., L. R., 3 C. P. 374, n.

"If a line becomes blocked up and impeded by snow, the company is bound to use all reasonable exertions to forward the passengers, although that may put the company to extra expense which of course they have no way of recovering from the travellers;[1] so I presume ere long extra engines and snow ploughs will come to our rescue."

"It is to be hoped that the fuel will last," said the lady. "How I pity those poor cattle that we heard lowing so plaintively as we passed them at the last siding," she added tenderly.

"Yes; no great efforts will be made for their convenience; if a snow-storm comes, the company is not bound to forward them by extraordinary means and at additional expense."[2]

"Poor things," said my fair companion, who seemed

> A very woman; full of tears,
> Hopes, blushes, tenderness, fears,
> Griefs, laughter, kindness, joys, and sighs,
> Loves, likings, friendships, sympathies;
> A heart to feel for every woe,
> And pity, if not dole, bestow.

"Poor things, unless in the hereafter there is a place where the spirits of animals be at rest, they have to bear a very heavy share of the primeval curse, and pay dearly for Adam's transgression and fall."

[1] Addison on Torts, 3d ed. 448.
[2] Briddon v. Gt. Northern Rw., 28 L. J., Ex. 51.

CHAPTER XII.

DUE CARE.

Snowed up. — Pacific Railway. — Passenger Carriers not Insurers. — Company must use Due Care. — Defective Machinery. — Broken Axle. — Company must account for Accident. — Difference between Goods and Men. — What is Due Care. — Latent Defects in Cars. — English Rule. — Rule in New York. — Moralizing. — Railroad Death-rate.

As the train came to a solemn pause in a deep cutting a number of us gathered together in the warm and cosy Pullman, the *ne plus ultra* of railway cars, far surpassing in comfort and luxury an English or Continental first-class carriage, though not adorned as are the Italian cars with those abominations of the sterner sex — tidies for the head to rest against. And here, each in turn related railroad adventures and accidents; tales which excited laughter and joyous merriment, of engagements, love scenes, marriage ceremonies, undress exhibitions in sleeping cars; tales of sorrow and grief, collisions, explosions, helpless people crushed, boiled, roasted to death; dozens plunged into eternity in a moment by the simple derangement of a switch, the starting of a rail, a flaw in a wheel, a sleepy pointsman, or a weary telegraph clerk.

One told that, in India, railroad traffic is seriously affected by the stagnation of the matrimonial market, a wedding there being an occasion of great pomp and the gathering together of friends; that the railways are breaking down the castes, as the conductors tumble into the same car proud, lofty, blue-blooded Brahmins, poor despised Pariahs, blood-thirsty Thugs, sun-worshipping Parsees, and learned Mussulmans; and go together these must, notwithstanding the dogmas of Shasters, Vedas, and Korans, or else jump out and die. Another told of having found nuggets of gold, the remains of melted jewelry, among the charred and blackened remains of unfortunates consumed at the Komoka (Ont.) accident. While a third in graphic terms described the efforts made to break through a snow blockade on the Central Pacific; the snow was a solid mass twenty feet high in front of the plough; ten engines were at work; they backed up about a mile, then reversing made a spring forward, locomotives shrieking and screeching, men yelling and gesticulating, volumes of smoke pouring forth from every funnel and hanging like a pall over the scene; the loud rumbling of the huge iron-beaked monster flying over the track, the hissing, roaring din and the chorus of shrieking demons behind made up a scene that would blanch the boldest cheek. With the force of a thousand giants the plough rushed upon the snow and hurled it in enormous masses, like mighty billows, down the mountain sides, crushing through the lofty pines, and glistening and gleaming like frosted silver as it fell upon the frozen cataract below; but the charge was well nigh in vain.

Thus with the flow of reason and the feast of soul passed some weary hours. At last, one gentleman turning to me, said: —

"I believe that a carrier of goods is liable for his freight in every event; is a carrier of passengers responsible to the same extent?"

"No," I responded, "all jurists are agreed that railway companies are only liable for negligence, either proximate or remote, and not for injuries happening to passengers from unforeseen accident or misfortune, where there has been no negligence or default on the part of the carrier;[1] still it is the bounden duty of a company to use due and proper care and skill in conveying travellers; and this duty laid upon them does not arise from any contract made between the company and the persons conveyed by them, but is one which the law imposes. If railways are bound to carry, they are also bound to carry safely; it is not sufficient for them to bring merely the dead body of their passenger to the end of the journey, and there deliver up the remains, parboiled or cut into sausage meat, to his executors and administrators.[2] The

[1] Aston *v.* Heaven, 2 Esp. 533; Frink *v.* Potter, 17 Ill. 406.
[2] Collett *v.* London & N. W. Rw., 16 Ad. & Ell. (N. S.), 984.

fact that injury is suffered by any one while upon the company's train, as a passenger, through any failure of the means of safe transportation, is regarded as *primâ facie* evidence of their liability;[1] and such evidence, if not rebutted by the company, will justify a verdict against them which a court will not set aside."[2] And having delivered myself of this harangue, I looked around with a self-satisfied air and rubbed my hands with invisible soap, in imperceptible water, *à la* Tom Hood.

"Yes," said an engineer, "a company is bound to use the best precautions in known practical use to secure the safety of their passengers,[3] but not every possible preventive which the highest scientific skill might have suggested,[4] nor every device which ingenuity might imagine.[5] But it appears hard that a company should be held liable — as they have been — for injuries arising from a crack in the axle of a car indiscoverable by any practical mode of examination,[6] and be bound to provide roadworthy carriages, absolutely and irrespectively of negligence."

"Yes, that is the rule in New York State, but

[1] Denman, C. J., in Carpue *v.* London & B. Rw., 5 Q. B. 747; Laing *v.* Colder, 8 Penn. St. 479-483.

[2] Dawson *v.* Manchester S. & L. Rw., 5 L. T. (N. S.), 682; but see Hammack *v.* White, 11 C. B. (N. S.), 587.

[3] Hegeman *v.* West. Rw. Corp., 16 Barb. 353.

[4] Ford *v.* London & S. W. R., 2 F. & F. 730, per Erle, C. J.

[5] Baltimore & Ohio Rw. *v.* State, 29 Md. 252.

[6] Alden *v.* N. Y. Central Rw., 26 N. Y. 102.

it has been somewhat questioned in later cases, and in fact it was laid down that a company is not responsible for injuries caused by *vis major*, as the breaking of a rail through extreme cold."[1]

"Wal, strangers," quoth a regular long, lean, lanky down-easter, "look ye har, down in my State, a carrier is bound to use the highest degree of care that a reasonable man would use."[2]

"That is substantially the same as the rule in the English cases," I said, "and has, I believe, been followed in most of the States, and in the United States Supreme Court."[3]

"I presume," said the machinist; "companies are liable for defects in their cars whether they manufacture them or purchase them?"

"Oh yes," I rejoined, "the companies are alike bound to see that in the construction no care or skill has been omitted for the purpose of making their engines and cars as safe as care and skill can make them."[4]

"I remember," spake the man of science, "hearing of one case where the engine ran off the track, and it was found that a fore-axle was broken, but no evidence was given as to whether the accident caused, or was caused by, the breakage; yet a traveller who had his shoulder contused, and his

[1] McPadden *v.* N. Y. C. Rw., 44 N. Y. 478; 47 Barb. 247.

[2] 13 Conn. 326.

[3] Redfield on Railways, vol. ii., 222 n.

[4] Hegeman *v.* Western Rw., 16 Barb. 353, affirmed by Court of Appeals, 13 N. Y. 9.

hat crushed, and was rendered insensible for a time and sick for a longer period by the accident, recovered a large sum against the company.[1] And in another English case[2] an accident happened from the breaking of the tire of a driving-wheel; the defect could not have been discovered by the original testing, but *might have* been if it had been repeated when the tire was returned after being considerably worn. The company was held liable. And so where the defect might have been discovered when the car was mended, and it was sent on without being thoroughly examined and repaired."[3]

"Yes," said one who had not yet spoken, "I was on a jury in a case against the Great Western of Canada. The axle of the tender had broken, and the tender and a car went off the track, and a man who was in the car had his arm broken. At the trial the company proved by the engineer in charge of the train, that he had examined the axle shortly before the accident and that all appeared in good order. The judge charged in favor of the defendants, but we found a verdict for the plaintiff, which the court refused afterwards to interfere with, as we were the proper judges as to whether or not there had been negligence on the part of the company."[4]

1 Dawson *v.* Manchester L. & L. Rw., 5 L. T. (N. S.), 682; see also, Skinner *v.* London B. & S. C. Rw., 5 Ex. 787; Carpue *v.* Same, 5 Ad. & E. (N. S.), 747; Bird *v.* Gt. Northern Rw. 28 L. J., Ex. 3.

2 Manser *v.* Eastern Counties Rw., 3 L. T. (N. S.), 585, Exch.

3 Richardson *v.* G. E. R., L. R., 10 C. P. 486; reversed on appeal, W. N. May 20, 1876.

4 Thatcher *v.* Gt. W. R., 4 U. C. C. P 543.

"I think that it was in that case that Chief Justice Macaulay remarked, that the accident having happened unaccountably, and without any proximate or active cause to account for it, constituting as the cases say some evidence of negligence, it rested with the company to explain and reconcile it with perfect innocence on their part. It has been held, too, in England, that the plaintiff is not bound to show specifically in what the negligence of the company consisted; but that if some inevitable fatality caused the accident, it is for the company to prove it.[1] In New York, too, the same view is taken."[2]

"Wal, stranger, what is yer law about this yer in the old country? Not that I care three shakes of a dead possum's tail about the old country, and all yer lawyers and judges with their horse-tail wigs, but still I calkerlate I kind o' like to know what they do say on this here point; as it appears to me that the great Amerikin eagle has got rather mixed up." And to add emphasis to his query, our friend of the land of wooden nutmegs fired from between his teeth a perfect *feu de joie* of extract of nicotine.

Thus appealed to, I cleared my throat, pulled up my shirt-collar, crossed my legs, assumed as authoritative an expression of countenance as Dame Nature ever permits me to do, and thus began:—

[1] Skinner *v.* London B. & S. C., 5 Ad. & E. (N. S.), 747.
[2] McPadden *v.* N. Y. C., 44 N. Y. 478.

"So long ago as the days of Sir James Mansfield it was held[1] that there is a decided difference between a contract to carry goods and one to carry passengers. In the former case the carrier is liable for his freight in any event, but he does not warrant the safety of his passengers. His undertaking as to them extends no further than this, that as far as human care and foresight can go he will provide for their safe conveyance. So, if the breaking of a coach is purely accidental the injured traveller will have no remedy for the misfortune he has encountered. The contract made by a general carrier of passengers is to take due care to carry his living freight safely; and it does not amount to a warranty that the carriage or car shall be in all respects perfect for its purpose, *i. e.*, free from all defects likely to cause a catastrophe, although those defects were such that no skill, care, or foresight could have detected their existence.[2] The obligation to use all due and proper care is founded on reasons obvious to any one with a semi-optic; but to impose on the carrier the burden of a warranty that everything he necessarily uses is absolutely without spot or blemish and free from defects likely to cause peril — when from the nature of things defects must exist which no skill can detect, and the effects of which no care or foresight can avert — would be to compel a man

[1] Christie *v.* Griggs, 2 Camp. 79.

[2] Readhead *v.* Midland Rw., L. R., 4 Q. B. 379, Ex. Ch.; also, L. R., 2 Q. B. 412, and the cases therein cited.

by implication of law and not by his own will to promise the performance of an impossible thing, and would be directly opposed to the maxims of law, 'Lex non cogit ad impossibilia,' 'Nemo tenetur ad impossibilia.' [Here the audience coughed.] 'Due care,' however, undoubtedly means (having reference to the nature of the contract to carry) a high degree of care, and casts on carriers the duty of exercising all vigilance to see that whatever is required for the safe conveyance of their passengers is in fit and proper order. But the duty to take due and proper care, however widely construed, however vigorously enforced, will not, as that man Readhead sought to do, subject a railway company to the plain injustice of being compelled by law to make reparation for a disaster arising from a latent defect in the machinery which they are obliged to use, which no human skill or care could have prevented or detected, or eye descried unless of 'the patent double million magnifyin' gas microscopes of hextra power kind' to which Mr. Weller, Jr., refers. In that case, the accident was caused by the breaking of the tire of one of the wheels of the carriage, owing to a latent defect in it, which was not attributable to any fault on the part of the manufacturers, nor was it discoverable previously to the breakage. The rule laid down in that case (Readhead's) seems to be that although the carrier of passengers may be responsible for deficiencies caused by want of skill or care in the manufacture of the carriages used, he is not to be so held when the defect could not have been avoided in the making, or detected on examination. It is so extremely improbable that such a case should happen, that the practical difference between this and the New York rule of absolute responsibility[1] is not of much importance, although the theoretical difference is. But the rule in New York does not seem to be fully approved of even on this side of the Atlantic.[2] The truth seems to be that carriers of persons must be held to the utmost degree of care, vigilance, and precaution, but not to such a degree of vigilance as would be wholly inconsistent with the mode of conveyance adopted and render it impracticable. Nor is the utmost degree of care which the human mind is capable of imagining required. Such a rule would require such an expenditure of money and employment of hands so as to render everything safe, as would prevent all persons of ordinary prudence from engaging in that kind of business. But the rule does necessitate that the highest degree of practicable care and diligence that is consistent with the mode of transportation adopted, should be used." [3]

I stopped; one universal sigh of relief uprose

[1] Alden *v.* New York Central Rw., 26 N. Y. 102.

[2] McPadden *v.* N. C., 44 N. Y. 478; Meier *v.* Penn. Rw., 64 Penn. St. 225, and Ingalls *v.* Bills, 9 Met. 1, where the court said, "If the injury arise from some invisible defect which no ordinary test will disclose, the carrier is not liable."

[3] ...ller *v.* Talbot, 23 Ill. 357.

from those of my listeners who were not nodding approvingly from the borders of Dreamland. The Yankee said: —

"Wal, stranger, that was a yarn. I guess I'll go and have a smoke, and see if I can calkerlate what in blazes you did mean by all that long pow-wow." And he departed.

"I think," said the juror, "that the law ought to be the most stringent possible in order to put a stop to such barbarous and inhuman sacrifice of multitudes, such horrible mangling of bodies and limbs, such frightful cases of burning alive and scalding to death that have occurred so frequently of late."

"Yes, I hope that the day is not very far distant when all our courts will hold, that all who undertake the transportation of passengers by the dangerous element of steam, and with the great speed of railway trains, are responsible for the use of every precaution which any known skill or experience has yet been able to devise, and that passengers need not judge for themselves how many of these precautions it is safe to forego."[1]

"But," urged another, "people now-a-days wish cheap and rapid travelling in all directions and everywhere."

"Suppose they do; we do not allow monomaniacs or brigands to commit suicide or murder without interference, because it is their pleasure

[1] Redfield on Railways, vol. ii., p. 237.

or their interest to do so; and I see no good reason why railway passengers or railway managers should be allowed to roast a hecatomb in human sacrifice, because it seems desirable or convenient to the one or the other class concerned in the immolation, or because the one class demands and the other consents, to use a mode of transportation which inevitably produces these results." [1]

"Ah," said a lady, "I fear these dreadful accidents will continue until every train is compelled to carry a director of the company, or a general manager, upon the cow-catcher; experience will then soon induce them to be a little more careful of the bodies and lives of others."

"But, sir!" said the scientific gentleman, a precise man of figures, "I fear you exaggerate when you speak of hecatombs of sacrifices. I believe that in proportion to the numbers carried the accidents to passengers in the good old days of stage-coaches were, as compared with these days of railway dispensation, about as sixty to one. Reliable statistics in France prove this. Figures, which you know are proverbial for their truth, show that absolutely more travellers were yearly killed and injured, without fault of theirs, fifty years ago on stage-coaches, than are now killed on the cars. According to the Report of the Board of Trade of Great Britain and Ireland, out of all the 480,000,000 of journeys taken by pas-

[1] Redfield on Railways, vol. ii., p. 238.

sengers by rail in the British Isles in 1874, only 212 people were killed, and 1,990 injured not fatally; so that you can easily see only one solitary traveller was killed to every 2,274,881 who followed in the triumphant train of the iron horse, and only one injured to every 242,301 passengers."

"You speak only of passengers," said a listener. "I presume far more employees were killed during that time."

"Certainly. Only 212 passengers were killed that year while as many as 788 employees were; and of the injured ones 1,990 paid for the privilege, while 2,815 were paid for running the risk: and of these mangled ones many had only themselves to blame. Sir John Hawkshaw, an authority on these matters, recently asserted that railway accidents were fewer now than ever: that in fact, on an average, a man might travel 100,000 miles each year for forty years, and the chances would be slightly in favor of his not receiving the smallest scratch, unless he ran into danger of his own accord."

"You might almost as well at once assert that it is less dangerous to travel by rail than to stay at home," I remarked.

"That very statement was officially made in France some years ago, and supported by the proof, that while ten people were killed on the rail, fourteen died at home from falling over carpets, and having their garments catch fire."

"All that may be true enough of England, or Europe; but I should think that it was widely different in America," I replied.

"Of course it must be admitted that, taken as a whole, the dangers incident to railway travelling are materially greater in America than in any country of Europe. Still the destruction of life and limb is nothing frightful, — the wonder rather is that so few are hurt. Perhaps you will not believe it, yet the truth of the fact remains, that in the year 1874, throughout the whole of Massachusetts, but one passenger was killed on the cars through an accident to which his own carelessness did not contribute; while in the same year of grace, in the city of Boston alone, fifteen people were killed from falling down stairs, twelve by falling out of windows, and seventeen were run over by carriages and fatally injured."

"But perhaps, that was an exceptional year!"

"Let us take four years then, from September, 1870, to the same month of 1874: in that time the railroads disposed of 635 persons, all told, passengers, employees, trespassers — in Massachusetts; and in Boston during the same years there were 1,050 accidental deaths! The returns for the last fifteen years show, that in Massachusetts only 39 passengers were killed, while 250 were injured, but not fatally, from causes over which they had no control: that is less than one killed to each 8,900,000 travellers, and about one in each

1,400,000 injured. The statistics for that State would appear to indicate that if one chanced to be born on a train and remained there travelling 500 miles a day, he would, with average good fortune, be about two hundred and twenty years old before being involved in any accident resulting in death, or personal injury."

"That is quite long enough, since Methusaleh is no more."[1]

[1] See "Our Railroad Death-rate," in Atlantic Monthly for February, 1876, by C. F. Adams, Jr.

CHAPTER XIII.

ACCIDENTS TO TRAVELLERS.

Standing on Platforms of Cars. — Room and Seats to be Furnished. — Over-crowding. — Riding in Express Cars. — In Caboose Car. — Rule in Illinois. — Walking through the Train. — Innocent Blood. — Damages to Infants and Juveniles. — Child's Fare Unpaid. — $1,800 for a Baby's Leg and Hand. — Negligence of a Nurse. — Travelling on Free Pass. — Conditional Liability. — Company Exempt. — Pat and Sambo. — Home again from a Foreign Shore.

OUR Connecticut friend went out of the car and stood on the platform, in defiance of the notice posted up on the door forbidding people to stand there; and gazing out into the storm and the night, he tried, like sister Ann, to distinguish whether there were any signs of relief coming to us in our benighted condition. As he, an omnivorous, breeches-wearing biped, balanced himself on his long slender legs and stretched forward his lean and lank corpus to look ahead, the engine gave a sudden puff and plunge, Conn. lost his balance and fell to the ground: the snow prevented much damage happening to his fragile body, but unfortunately his foot rested partly on the rail, and the wheel of the car badly crushed his big toe. The violent ear-piercing howls that issued from his tobacco-seasoned throat brought assistance very soon, and he was speedily helped back into the car; his damaged pedal member was dressed by a young member of the Æsculapian fraternity who chanced to be on board and seemed eager to show his surgical skill.

The injured man soon became violent in his denunciations of the carelessness of the company, in his threats of vengeance in the form of suits for damages. He was, however, suddenly checked in the outpouring of the vials of his wrath by one of the passengers remarking: —

"Perhaps you do not know that in these hyperborean regions people can claim no compensation for injuries received while on the platform of a car (or on any baggage, wood, or freight car), in violation of the printed regulations posted up conspicuously, and where there is proper and ample accommodation for the passengers inside the car."[1]

"And there is a similar statute in New York State," added another.[2]

"Yes," I said, "no one can recover for an injury of which his own negligence was in the whole, or in part, the proximate cause."[3]

"Wal, but the old conductor saw me thar and did n't say nothink agin' it," quoth the wounded man.

"That makes no difference.[4] If there had been

[1] Railway Act, 1868, s. 20, sub-sec. 13 (Canada).
[2] Redfield on Railways, vol. ii., p. 252.
[3] Robinson *v.* Cone, 22 Vt. 213; Butterfield *v.* Forrester, 11 East, 60.
[4] Higgins *v.* N. Y. & Harlem Rw., 2 Bosw. 132.

no notice up you might get something out of them."[1]

"I think," I said, "that it has been held, in one case at least, to be a question for the jury, whether the passenger had notice not to stand outside, and whether the fact of his disregarding it contributed to the injury; and they having failed to find these facts, the Court of Appeals let the plaintiff keep the $10,000, awarded him."[2]

"Oh, Jee-ru-sa-lem and Jee-ri-cho, I go in for that slick and quick," cried the victim at the sound of the almighty dollars.

"Ha-ha; but the company, if you sue them, will only have to show that there was room and an unoccupied seat inside the cars for you. Of course, one is not obliged to displace either the persons or property of other passengers, or urge them to give up half a seat, or even a whole one, needlessly occupied by them;[3] that is the duty of the conductor; nor is one obliged to sit in the smoking car."[4]

"But," asked a lady, "should a passenger go through all the train searching for a place wherein to bestow her weary frame?"

"No; it is no compliance with the duty of the company to provide proper accommodation, that

[1] Colegrove v. N. Y. & N. H. Rw., 6 Duer, 382.

[2] Zemp v. W. & M. Rw., 9 Rich., 84.

[3] Robinson v. Fitchburg & Worcester Rw., 7 Gray, 92; Willis v. Long Island Rw., 34 N. Y. 670; Bass v. C. & N. W. Rw., 36 Wis. 461.

[4] Bass v. C. & N. W. Rw., *supra*.

there is sufficient room in a carriage remote from the place where the passenger was allowed to enter.[1] C. J. Coleridge once remarked in the hearing of a friend of mine, that there may be no negligence in the company's servants allowing too many persons to get into a carriage, as it would be difficult at all times to prevent it, and perhaps there would be no help for it until the arrival at the next station. But permitting an extra number to remain in the car and to continue to impose undue restraint and discomfort upon the other passengers is evidence of negligence; and companies should have a sufficient number of attendants at each station to see that their cars are not overcrowded."[2]

"How would it be where a passenger is in the baggage car with the knowledge of the conductor, and is there injured?" asked one.

"It was decided in Canada, in such a case, that the traveller could recover damages. There a man went into the express company's compartment (which was not intended for passengers, but whither they oft times resorted to smoke the pipe of peace): a notice was usually put upon the inside of the doors of the passenger cars and on the outside of the door of the baggage car, forbidding travellers to ride in the latter, but it was not shown that it was there on that particular day;

[1] Willis v. Long Island Rw., 34 N. Y., 670.
[2] Jackson v. Metropolitan Rw., L. R., 10 C. P. 49.

the conductor passed through the car twice while the man was in there and made no objection. By a collision, this Watson had an arm broken, while none of those in the passenger car were much hurt, and the court held that even if W. was aware of the notices, yet the company were not thereby excused, under the circumstances.[1] But where a man rode free of charge on an engine, after the engineer had told him that it was against the rules for him to do so, it was held that he was a wrong-doer, and could not recover for injuries sustained while he bestrode the iron horse, as the consent of the engineer conferred no legal right.[2] If, however, passengers are carried, and charged fare, in the caboose car (whatever that may be) of freight trains, they have the same right to be conveyed safely as if luxuriating in a gorgeous Pullman palace car,[3] and so where one rides on a gravel train.[4] And where the conductor, though against the rules, allowed a passenger to travel in a freight car, charging him a first-class fare, the company were held to have incurred the same liability for his safety as if he had been in a regular passenger train.[5] Ditto where the conductor of a coal

[1] Watson *v.* Northern Rw. Co., 24 U. C. Q. B. 98; see also, Carroll *v.* N. Y. & N. H. Rw., 1 Duer, 571, where a man took a seat in the post office department of baggage car with the assent of the conductor.

[2] Robertson *v.* N. Y. & E. Rw., 22 Barb, 91.

[3] Edgerton *v.* N. Y. & H. Rw., 39 N. Y. St. 227; Indianapolis, etc., *v.* Beaver, 41 Ind. 497.

[4] Lawrenceburgh & Upper Miss. Rw. *v.* Montgomery, 7 Ind. 474.

[5] Dunn *v.* G. T. Rw., 10 Am. Law Reg. (N. S.), 615.

train invited a man to take a ride and charged him naught." [1]

"That may be true enough down east, but out west if a passenger takes a freight train he takes it with the increased risk and diminution of comfort incident thereto, and if it is managed with the care requisite for such trains, it is all he has a right to expect or demand;" [2] remarked one who hailed from the city of Widow O'Leary's celebrated cow.

"By the way," said a gentleman, who had been listening attentively to all the conversation; "can any of you gentlemen, who seem to have the whole law appertaining to railways at your finger's ends or the tips of your tongues (whichever expression be the more correct or implies the greater knowledge), tell me whether it is safe for one to promenade from one end of the train to the other for the sake of exercise or to see who is on board? Down in New York State the jury must decide whether it is right so to do, in order to find a seat." [3]

"Out west," said the Chicagoian, "It has been decided that passengers have no right to pass from car to car, unless for some reasonable purpose; [4] and heaven only knows what twelve enlightened men from the body of the country would, in their wisdom, deem to be reasonable."

1 Eaton *v.* Del., Lack., & W. Rw., 1 Am. Law Record, 121; 57 N. Y. 382.

2 Chicago, B., & Q. Rw. *v.* Hazzard, 26 Ill. 373.

3 McIntyre *v.* N. Y. Central Rw., 37 N. Y. 287.

4 Galena & Chicago Rw. *v.* Yarwood, 15 Ill. 468.

"Humph, you don't seem to have a very high opinion of juries," said the representative of that class, who had already joined in the conversation.

"I rather think not; who could, when they elaborate such queer decisions from their brains and shew such ignorance. I know one case where an intelligent jury brought in a verdict of 'guilty' against the plaintiff in a libel suit; of another, where, at the close of a lengthy trial, the foreman coolly asked the judge to explain 'two terms of law, namely plaintiff and defendant.' Many of them would be decidedly improved were occasional punishment inflicted as in the good old days of yore, when sometimes a juryman was fined and had his nose split; and the usual fate of a disagreeing jury was to be put into a cart and shot into the nearest ditch."

Our train had been released from bondage and under weigh for some time, and just at this juncture the conversation was stopped by a collision taking place. Fortunately the drivers of the approaching engines had discovered the danger some time previously; they were, therefore, enabled by putting on the breaks so to deaden the speed that the trains barely touched each other — gently kissed, as it were — and although some of the passengers were jerked forward in an uncomfortable manner as if they had been suddenly punched in a sensitive part, still no persons were seriously hurt except two. One of these unfortunates was the newsboy, who in passing from one car to another was thrown to the ground and had a leg badly crushed; the other was a beautiful little child of some three or four summers who had been playing with a lady and was knocked violently down, and in falling hit his head against the side of a seat. From his pure white forehead a purple stream was slowly trickling, dyeing his golden ringlets, as he lay unconscious upon his weeping mother's knee. While some tried to restore the child, and others to console the parent, I took a business-like view of the transaction, and "with all the homage due to a sex of which I am enthused dreadful," as Col. Morley of the Parisians would say, I approached and said, —

"Madam, each drop of that child's blood is worth money; you may lay the foundation of his future fortune now in the days of his youth by recovering damages against the company for the injury they have done to him;" she heeded not, but I continued. "Why, in one case a child two years old was wandering on a track and being run over by a train lost a leg and a hand, and the jury gave it $1,800;[1] why, that sum put out at compound interest would — "

"Oh, you horrid man," exclaimed the mother, "to talk that way. But I did not buy a ticket for him, and I should have, as he is over three years old." And the mother's grief broke out

[1] Redfield on Railways, vol. ii., p. 243, n.; Rauch *v.* Lloyd, 31 Penn. St. 358.

afresh, as she thought she had lost this golden opportunity.

"Don't trouble yourself, madam, that makes no difference, the contract made with you when you bought your ticket was that both you and your child should be carried safely, and if there was any misrepresentation on your part as to the little sufferer's age, although it might render you liable for the fare that should have been paid, or for a penalty, still it does not alter the position of the company, and they were and are bound to carry you and the little dear safely." [1]

"Ah!" sighed the mother, "if that nasty woman had only held him up, and not have let him fall, — perhaps the jury will say she ought to have done so?"

I was glad to see that the thought of the almighty dollar was applying a golden salve to the mother's wounded heart, if not to the boy's forehead, for I hate tears, crocodile or otherwise, and was therefore willing to enlighten her ladyship as much as possible, especially as I make it a constant practice to give advice gratuitously (when I think it won't be paid for), and putting down the usual charge for it to the account of my charitable disbursements; so I said: —

"The misconduct of one assuming to take charge of a child, but to whom it has not been entrusted, will not preclude a recovery on its part

[1] Austin *v.* Gt. Western Rw., L. R., 2 Q. B. 442.

for the negligence of the company.[1] In fact many of the American courts hold that no amount of negligence on the part of parents and guardians will excuse those injuring a child;[2] especially, if the action for such injury is brought by the child and not by the parents to recover damages for the death of their little one." [3]

Alas, for the poor mother's peace of mind, there was a Job's comforter on board, and he opened his mouth, and although he did not bray as he should have done, being what he was, he spake thus: —

"The law in the State of Massachusetts is that the negligence of those who have the charge of children, or invalids, unable to take care of themselves, will injuriously affect their right of action." [4]

"Thank goodness we are not near the Hub of the universe now," I exclaimed, sharply.

"And very much the same rule is laid down in England, and in the States of Maine, New York and Indiana.[5] In England where a child five years old was in the charge of his grandmother and was injured by a train while crossing the track, it was held that he was so identified with his old granny that on account of her careless-

[1] N. Penn. Rw *v.* Mahoney, 57 Penn. St. 187.

[2] Wharton on Negligence, § 310.

[3] N. P. Rw. *v.* Mahoney, *supra;* B. & I. Rw. *v.* Snyder, 18 Ohio St. 399.

[4] Holly *v.* Boston Gas Light Co., 8 Gray, 123; Wright *v.* Malden & M. Rw., 4 Allen, 283.

[5] Wharton on Negligence, § 311

ness an action in his name could not be maintained against the company.[1] And where a passing train cut off the leg of a three and a half year old child, the court considered that the company were not responsible, unless it was shown that he had strayed upon the track through their negligence or default.[2] And in the United States it has been held that to allow an infant, four years old, to wander at its own sweet will in the public streets, is such negligence on the part of the parents as will prevent the child recovering for any damages sustained.[3]

"But not if the child were six, and the street a quiet one"[4] — I broke in, but my adversary continued: —

"Or to suffer a child of two summers to cross a street traversed by a horse-railway."[5]

"But a five year old may cross such a street,"[6] I again broke in.

"Or even to cross a street and go a few yards down to its house."[7] Here he stopped.

"I have read somewhere that in England they take more pains to protect an oyster than a child,"[8] remarked one of the listeners.

1 Waite *v.* N. E. Rw., El. Bl. & El. 719.
2 Singleton *v.* Eastern C. Rw., 7 C. B. N. S. 287.
3 Mangam *v.* Brooklyn, etc., Rw., 36 Barb. 230.
4 Cosgrove *v.* Ogden, 49 N. Y. 255; see Karr *v.* Parks, 40 Cal. 188.
5 Wright *v.* Malden & M. Rw., 4 Allen, 283.
6 Barksdull *v.* N. O. & C. R., 23 La. An. 180.
7 Callahan *v.* Bean, 9 Allen, 401.
8 Wharton on Negligence, § 312.

"Never mind his croaking, madam," I went on. "These cases he mentions do not apply to you. If they did it would be visiting the sins of the fathers upon the children to an extent not contemplated by the decalogue (as a judge once remarked),[1] and, besides, on this side of the water a parent may suffer a child four years old to cross a street by itself to school;[2] or wander about a station,[3] without freeing the company from liability."

"Ditto down where I growed;"[4] interruptingly ejaculated our Connecticut friend.

"Parents," I added, "need only be ordinarily careful in not allowing their small fry to get into danger.[5] But I must go and see the newsboy."

Off I started instanter —

> For a virtuous action should never be delayed,
> The impulse comes from heaven, and he who strives
> A moment to repress it, disobeys
> The god within his mind.

I found the youth in the baggage car with his leg tightly bandaged. The pallor spread over his countenance, the beads of perspiration on his brow, and his closely pressed lips, told that his sufferings were great; but with Spartan courage he repressed every voluntary sign of pain. A group of rough, yet tender men were gathered round him,

1 Lannen *v.* Albany Gas Light Co., 46 Barb. 264.
2 Lynch *v.* Smith, 104 Mass. 52.
3 Stout *v.* S. C. & P. Rw., 11 Am. Law Reg. (N. S.), 226
4 Daley *v.* Norwich & W. Rw., 26 Conn. 591.
5 P. A. & M. Rw. *v.* Pearson, 72 Penn. St. 169

and they told me that it was feared he would have to lose his leg; that he was the only son of his mother, and she was a widow with no stay nor support save the earnings of her boy.

"I say, mister," said one of the party to me, "I kind of calculate you are a lawyer from what I heard you say before we left the station, and I want to know whether a man who has not got a a ticket can sue the railway for damages."

I replied, "Every person is a passenger and entitled to be carried safely (so far as due care will provide for his safety), who is lawfully on the train;[1] and the *onus* is on the company to prove affirmatively that he is a trespasser.[2] Any one permitted to ride in a train as a passenger is entitled to demand and expect the same immunity from peril whether he pay for his seat or no; the confidence induced is a sufficient legal consideration to create a duty in the performance of the service undertaken;[3] so, if one is injured by the culpable negligence or want of skill of the company's servants he is entitled to recover although he is a dead-head.[4] Thus, a newspaper reporter travelling on a free ticket—even if granted to another brother of the press;[5] the president of of one company riding by request of the president

1 Gt. Western of Canada *v.* Braid, 1 Moore P. C. (N. S.), 101.

2 Penn. Rw. Co. *v.* Books, 7 Am. Law Reg. (N. S.), 524.

3 Coggs *v.* Bernard, Holt, 13.

4 Ohio & Miss. Rw. *v.* Muhling, 30 Ill. 9.

5 Gt. Northern Rw. *v.* Harrison, 12 C. B. 576; Gillenwater *v.* Madison & Indian Rw., 5 Ind. 340.

of another;[1] a mail-clerk travelling in charge of the mail bags,[2] and a child for whom no fare has been paid;[3] were all held entitled to damages when injured. Nor — though this is rather beside the matter — does the fact that the train has been hired for an excursion excuse the negligence, or remove the liability of the company."[4]

"All right," said the man to the boy; "cheer up, sonny; you will get a pot of money for this that will keep you like a fighting-cock till you get round again."

"I did not say that," I remarked, gloomily shaking my head.

"Why, what do you mean?" was anxiously queried by several.

"Railway companies may stipulate for exemption from all responsibility for losses accruing to passengers from the negligence of their servants, unless, indeed, it arise from their fraudulent, reckless or wilful misconduct;[5] and where it has been agreed that, in consideration of a free pass, the passenger should travel at his own risk, or where he takes a free ticket having an express condition printed thereon 'whereby the holder assumes all

1 Phil. & Read. Rw. v. Derby, 14 How. (U. S.), 483.

2 Collett v. London & N. W. R., 16 Ad. & El. (N. S.) 984; Nolton v. Western R., 10 How. Pr. R. 97.

3 Austin v. Gt. Western Rw., L. R., 2 Q. B. 442.

4 Skinner v. London, B., & S. C. Rw., 5 Ex. 787; Cleveland, C. & C. Rw. v. Terry, 8 Ohio (N. S.), 570; but see Peoria Br. Ass. v. Loomis, 20 Ill. 235.

5 Welles v. N. Y. C., 26 Barb. 641; Indiana Central Rw. v. Mundy, 21 Ind. 48.

risk of accidents and expressly agrees that the company shall not be liable under any circumstances, whether of negligence by their agents or otherwise, for an injury to the person, or for any loss of or injury to the property,' such agreement or condition is good, and will exclude all liability on the part of the company for any negligence (save gross or wilful)[1] for which they would otherwise have been liable. That has been held in Canada;[2] in New York State,[3] in other States, and in England the company is not even liable for wilful or gross negligence.[4] The words "travel at his own risk" include all the incidents connected with the journey; all those risks which arise during the transit and until the transit is actually at an end, are guarded by these words. So if a man, whose ticket is thus marked after leaving the train and while going off the company's premises fall over a parapet and is injured, he will not be able to recover;[5] I mean to recover damages. But of course such an agreement does not extend to an independent wrong, as an assault or false imprisonment, or any rights as to criminal proceedings,[6]

[1] Ind. Cent. Rw. *v.* Mundy, 21 Ind. 48; Welles *v.* N. Y. C. Rw., 26 Barb. 641; Bissell *v.* N. Y. C., 29 Barb. 602; Ill. C. R. v. Read, 37 Ill. 484.

[2] Sutherland *v.* Gt. W. Rw., 7 U. C. C. P. 409; Woodruff *v.* G. W. R., 18 U. C. Q. B. 420.

[3] Welles *v.* N. Y. C., 26 Barb. 641.

[4] McCawley *v.* Furness Rw., L. R., 8 Q. B. 57.

[5] Gallin *v.* L. & N. W. Rw., L. R., 10 Q. B. 212; Hall *v.* N. E. Rw., L. R. 10 Q. B. 437.

[6] Ibid.

nor where the traveller is carried under an agreement between the company and some third party which says nothing about the traveller taking the risk himself."[1]

"What 's the use in such a long palaver," rudely interrupted my questioner, "the boy had no ticket at all."

"Well, where a newsboy of the name of Billy Alexander, while on the platform of a station, was struck by a piece of wood projecting from a passing car and so hurt that he died, it was held to be a good defence that he was a newsboy in the employ of Chisholm, selling papers on the company's trains under an agreement between Chisholm and the company, that the latter should not be liable for any injury to the newsboys or their goods, whether occasioned by the company's negligence or otherwise."[2]

"Do you mean to tell me," cried a listener, indignantly, "that in this free land of ours the life of a child can thus be sold by his employer?"

"Ah," I returned, "that is a question which Richards, C. J., did not decide. But if you want to know anything more on the subject call on me at my office, and I shall be most happy to attend to you," I added, as I left the car.

I now retired to my berth in the Pullman, where the company was bound to keep both my-

[1] Woodruff *v.* G. W. R., 18 U. C. Q. B. 420.

[2] Alexander *v.* Toronto & N. Rw., 33 U. C. Q. B. 474; *S. C.*, on appeal, 35 U. C. Q. B. 453.

self and my goods in safety while I slept.[1] I was scarcely settled there ere I heard loud and angry voices proceeding from the front end of the car, and recognized our Hamitic conductor's tones in the words —

"I tell you, sah, this is a sleeping car, and you can't come in without a ticket."

"Shure and I had a ticket, and its after slaping I want to be;" was the response in Milesian accents, broad and sweet.

"Whar is it?"

"Shure and I have lost the plaguy thing."

"If you have lost your ticket, sah, can you remember your berth?" asked the African.

A solemn pause, during which Paddy ruminated deeply, then he exclaimed,

"Och, by jabers, it is a hard thing to remember that, though I know I was there at the time; and my ould mother, rest her bones, tould me that I was born on Patrick's day in the morning, the year afore the famine, and more by token our old sow had a fine litter of pigs that selfsame day."

When the burst of laughter that greeted this reply had died away, I quickly subsided into the "arms of Murphy," and knew nothing more of railroads, railroad-law, or railroad travelling, until I was called by the descendant of Noah's naughty son, and informed that we were just at the station which I had left some days previously, and where

[1] Palmater v. Wagner, Marine Ct. N. Y. 1875.

my journeyings were for a time to end, and from which in a few minutes I would be transported to the bosom of my beloved spouse. Right glad was I when once again I stood — *mens sana in corpore sano* — on the platform of the depot of my native city, and saw the cabby coming from the baggage car with my traps on his brawny shoulder. I will draw the veil of modesty over the reception that awaited me at home, and where I soon showed myself to be "a forked straddling animal with bandy legs," as Dean Swift puts it; or as Sir John Falstaff, Knight, would say, "for all the world like a forked radish with a head fantastically carved upon it with a knife."

CHAPTER XIV.

INJURIES TO PASSENGERS AND EMPLOYEES.

An Inefficient Line. — Passengers hurt. — Employees killed. — Lord Campbell's Act. — Compensation for Death. — Solatium for Feelings Wounded. — Scotch Law. — American Law. — Hen-pecked Husband's Will. — The Rule in Massachusetts. — In Pennsylvania. — In Maryland. — In Canada. — Hard to decide. — Annuity Tables. — Bad or Diseased. — Insured. — Children Injured. — Parents Compensated. — Amounts obtained. — A Leg at $24,700. — For what compensated. — Chances of Matrimony. — Servants injured. — Fellow Servants. — Different Companies. — Which One to sue. — Strangers' Act. — Greedy Ruminant.

I HAD fondly hoped that no new points, quirks, or quiddities on railway law would arise in the course of my not very extensive practise for some time to come, so that I might have leisure to paddle my own little canoes, and issue little billets-doux in the Queen's name to the company on my own account. But alas! I had scarcely settled down in my office on the day of my arrival at home when my young friend, Tom Jones (to whom I referred in the early pages of this interesting and instructive diary of mine), came rushing in.

After a considerable amount of small talk, chit-chat and mutual inquiries after mutual friends and affairs, and things mutually interesting, Tom exclaimed, " I say, old fellow, I have a couple of matters that are bothering me, and I want your advice thereon."

By the way, nearly all Tom Jones' matters bothered him, and when they bothered him he bothered me, for he was not one of those who

> Make law their study and delight,
> Read it by day and meditate by night.

"All right," I said, extending my left digits towards him for an *honorarium*.

"Oh, I am not going to pay you," he remarked coolly, "so you need not expect it."

"Ah, well," I returned, quietly and with the air of an ill-used man, "I shall do like old Thurlow did, he could never come to a decision without a fee, and so when he had to decide upon some matter for himself he would take a guinea out of one pocket and put it into another. Now what are your questions?" I always preferred answering his queries to lending him books, for although he was a miserable hand at accounts he was a most excellent book-keeper.

"I suppose you know," began T. J., "that a short time ago, owing to a heavy storm, part of the line of the Blank Railway gave way"——

"That is *primâ facie* evidence of the insufficiency of its construction; and a company is bound to build its works in such a manner as that they will be capable of resisting all extremes of weather, which in the climate through which the line runs might be expected, though rarely, to occur. So say that august assembly, the Judicial Committee of the Privy Council."[1]

"Can't you wait a bit — that's not the point at all;" said Jones.

"Go on then."

"Several men were killed, and, as is usual, they all had large families of small children. Three of the wives have come to me to see if I can get damages against the company for them."

"Were they passengers or employees, for that makes a great difference," I said.

"One was employed on the line, the others were not," replied Tom.

"Well, let us settle about the others first."

"Well, what do you do first to get your damages? I mean under what Act do you proceed?"

"Under what in England is called Lord Campbell's Act (9 & 10 Vic. ch. 93), the Canadian Act[2] is a transcript of that; and a similar statute has been introduced into most of the States of the Union, to obviate that most heathenish of maxims *actio personalis moritur cum personam.* Our Act provides that when death shall be caused by the wrongful act, neglect or default, of any person, such as would (if death had not ensued) have entitled the party to an action, in every such case an action may be maintained by the executor or

[1] Gt. Western Rw. *v.* Fawcett; Same *v.* Braid, 1 Moore, P. C. C. (N. S.), 101; 9 Jur. (N. S.), 339.
[2] Con. Stat. Can. ch. 78.

administrator of the party injured, and the jury may give such damages as shall be proportioned to the injury resulting from the death of such party, to be divided among the members of his family as the jury shall direct. But, of course, if any negligence of the party himself, or those in charge of him, contribute directly to the injury, there can be no remedy.[1] Have twelve months elapsed since the death?"

"No," was the response.

"All right."

"What damages shall I claim?"

"Only such as will compensate for the pecuniary loss sustained,"[2] I returned.

"But one of my wives — the richest one, too, — went into most awful fits over the death of her husband, and has not been quite *compos mentis* since; and I want something to solace her for her mental sufferings."

"You cannot get it in this country, nor could you in England either. If the jury were to inquire into the degree of mental anguish which each member of a family suffers from a bereavement, then not only the child without filial piety, but a lunatic child and one of very tender years, and a posthumous child, on the death of the father, although getting something for pecuniary loss, would not come *in pari passu* with other

[1] Willets *v.* Buffalo & Rochester Rw., 14 Barb. 385, where a lunatic was left by himself and in consequence was killed.

[2] Blake *v.* Midland Rw., 18 Q. B. 93; Bradburn *v.* G. W. R., L.R., 10 Ex. 3.

children, and would be cut off from the solatium. If a jury were to proceed to estimate the respective degrees of mental anguish of a widow and twelve children from the death of the pater-familias, a serious danger might arise of damages being given to the ruin of the defendants: especially would the damages be disastrous if all the relatives mentioned in the fifth section of the Imperial Act (the sixth of the Canadian), the father and the mother, grandfather and grandmother, stepfather and stepmother, grandson and granddaughter, stepson and stepdaughter, not only got compensation for their pecuniary losses, but solatiums for their shattered affections, blighted expectations and broken hearts." [1]

"That is too bad," said Jones, "for I am sure the Scotch law gives a solatium for wounded feelings, even where the death of the man, instead of being a loss, is a gain to the family, owing to his bankruptcy or dissipated habits." [2]

"Yes," I replied, "but the Scotch are always more liberal than other people; they grant a solatium to a man injured in his happiness and circumstances by the death of his wife and child, whereas in England a widower will not get anything unless the death of his spouse causes him some pecuniary loss; [3] it being a pure question of

1 Blake *v.* Midland Rw., 18 Ad. & Ell. (N. S.), 93; Pym *v.* Great Northern Rw., 4 B. & S. (Ex. Ch.), 396.

2 Ersk. Inst. 592, note 13.

3 In argument Gillard *v.* Lancaster & Yorkshire Rw. Co., 12 L. T. 356.

pecuniary compensation, and nothing more, which is contemplated by the Act.[1] Nor, I believe, can a husband recover in New York State for the death of his wife.[2] But where the damages are for the next of kin, the services of the deceased mother in the nurture and instruction of her children, had she survived, may be properly considered.[3] I wonder what is the rule as to the solatium in the Republic — let us see."

So saying, I reached down a most useful book on Railways, by Chief Justice Redfield, of Vermont, and concerning "the great learning, research, and power of reasoning displayed" in which, Lord Chief Justice Cockburn speaks with expressions of admiration.

"Here it is: 'There seems no doubt, according to the best considered cases in this country, that the mental anguish which is the natural result of the injury, may be taken into account, in estimating damages to the party injured in such cases, although not of itself the foundation of an action.'"[4]

"It seems," remarked my friend, "somewhat strange that in Canada a person's feelings should make no difference; for one of my widows feels her

[1] Armsworth *v.* Southeastern Rw. Co., 11 Jurist, 758.

[2] Lucas *v.* N. Y. C., 21 Barb. 245; Worley *v.* Cincinnati, H., & D. Rw., 1 Handy, 481.

[3] Tilley *v.* Hudson River Rw., 29 N. Y. 252.

[4] Canning *v.* Williamstown, 1 Cush. 451; Morse *v.* Auburn & Syracuse Rw., 10 Barb. 623; so in California, Fairchild *v.* California Stage Co., 13 Cal. 599.

loss deeply, whereas the other is evidently one of those 'viders' against whom Samivel Veller, Senior, would have warned his hopeful boy."

"Both are entitled to the same compensation, although one was as closely joined in sympathy and spirit to her lost spouse as was Chang to Eng, in the flesh; and the other was the Elizabeth referred to in the will of that unfortunate wretch who died in London, in 1791. I must read you that will, though it is rather beside the subject, for it is a perfect model for hen-pecked husbands to follow; here it is. 'Seeing that I have had the misfortune to be married to the aforesaid Elizabeth, who ever since our union, has tormented me in every possible way; that heaven seems to have sent her into the world solely to drive me out of it; that the strength of Samson, the genius of Homer, the prudence of Augustus, the skill of Pyrrhus, the patience of Job, the philosophy of Socrates, the vigilance of Hermogenes, would not suffice to subdue the perversity of her character; that no power on earth can change her; seeing we have lived apart during the last eight years, and that the only result has been the ruin of my son, whom she has corrupted and estranged from me: weighing, maturely and seriously, all these considerations, I have bequeathed and I do bequeath, to my said wife Elizabeth, the sum of one shilling, to be paid to her within six months of my death.' But to return; as to damages, I see that in Massachusetts by statute[1] the passenger carrier is subject to a fine, not exceeding $5,000, to be recovered by indictment, to the use of the executor or administrator of the deceased for the benefit of his widow and heirs. Under this Act, if the death is instantaneous and simultaneous with the injury, as no right of action accrues to the person injured, there is none to which the Act can apply;[2] but it is sufficient if one does not die for fifteen minutes, although insensible from the first.[3] In Pennsylvania, the jury were told to estimate damages 'by the probable accumulations of a man of such age, habits, health, and pursuits as the deceased, during what would probably have been his lifetime.'[4] In Maryland the jury was directed to give such damages as would yield the family of the deceased the same support as they would have obtained from the labor of the father during the time he would probably have lived and worked, and that they might consider the age, health, and occupation of the man killed, and the comfort and support he was to his family at the time of his death."[5]

"I see," said Tom, who seemed unwilling that I should do all the talking, "that our own Chief Justice Robinson, on one occasion, confessed him-

[1] 1842, c. 89.
[2] Hollenbeck *v.* Berkshire Rw., 9 Cush. 481.
[3] Bancroft *v.* Boston & Worcester Rw., 11 Allen, 34.
[4] Penn. Rw. Co. *v.* McCloskey, 23 Penn. St. 526, 528.
[5] Baltimore & Ohio Rw. *v.* State, 24 Md. 271.

self utterly at a loss to make a satisfactory computation of the amount of damages to be awarded, or of the pecuniary loss sustained by a widow and her children through the death of the head of the house: he said he had no means of determining whether they would have been better off if the father's life had run its natural course, or not; it was mere conjecture. The father might have become extravagant or intemperate, and squandered his property; or from too great eagerness to grow rich, might have lost it by grasping at too much, or might have died from natural causes within a year or a month, leaving his family no better off than he did leave them when carried away by the sad accident.[1] And I think that I would be equally puzzled were I on a jury; I don't see how in the world a jury, except by drawing lots, can calculate the damages arising from the loss of the income, and of the care, protection, and assistance of the father."

"Yes, it must be rather a nice calculation."

"Suppose," continued Jones, "there was an accident to a train containing an archbishop, a lord chancellor, a bank director, a lunatic, a wealthy but immoral man, and one virtuous but bankrupt, and all these respectable persons came to final grief: how could any ordinary jury estimate the pecuniary value of the conjugal and paternal care, protection, and assistance of each of these."

[1] Secord *v.* Great Western Rw., 15 U. C. Q. B. 631.

"You need not put such an unlikely case," I said, "merely suppose that there were together one who —

'scorned life's mathematics,
Could not reckon up a score,
Pay his debts, or be persuaded
Two and two are always four.
That another was exact as Euclid,
Prompt and punctual, no one more.'

"Still," I added, "these difficult calculations have to be made."

"But how?"

"In England, it has been decided that the damages are not to be estimated according to the life of the man, calculated by annuity tables, but the jury should give what they consider a reasonable compensation;[1] although, in the United States, it was thought proper for the judge in charging the jury to allude to the expectation of life according to the tables deduced from the bills of mortality:[2] and even in England, in such cases, the average and probable duration of the life is a material point, which cannot be better shown than by the tables of insurance companies, who learn it by experience.[3] And the probable benefits of the continuance of the life of the father, as to the children, is to be estimated with reference to their majority, and as to the widow, with reference to

[1] Armsworth v. Southeastern Rw., 11 Jur. 759.

[2] Smith v. N. Y. & Harlem Rw., 6 Duer, 225; City of Chicago v. Major, 18 Ill. 349.

[3] Rowley v. London & N. W. Rw., 29 Law Times Rep. (N. S.), 180.

the expectation of life as determined by the tables.[1] Of course, the jury are not to attempt to give damages to the full amount of a perfect compensation for the pecuniary injury, but must take a reasonable view of the case, and give what they consider, under all the circumstances, a fair compensation."[2]

"Would it make any difference were the man of a bad character or diseased?"

"If the man had a fatal disease which would be sure to kill him in a short time, the amount of damages given should be less.[3] And as to character, the loss is supposed to be of a man as he ought to be. It has been held not to be necessary that the widow, or next of kin, should have any legal claim upon the deceased for support."[4]

"How would it be if he was insured, and by his death the family rather made than lost?"

"Well, I presume that if the insurance goes to a man's family, it would be a good reason for reducing the amount of damages. There appears to be only one English case on this point, and that was at *Nisi Prius* and is not reported at length; in it Lord Campbell told the jury to deduct from the amount of damages the amount of an insurance against accidents, and any reasonable sum

[1] Balt. & Ohio Rw. *v.* State, 33 Md. 542; Macon & Western Rw. *v.* Johnson, 38 Ga. 409.

[2] Rowley *v.* London & N. W. Rw., 29 Law Times Rep. (N. S.), 180.

[3] Birkett *v.* Whitehaven Junction Rw., 4 H. & N. 732.

[4] Railway Co. *v.* Barron, 5 Wallace, 90.

they should think fit in respect of life insurance.[1] In a Canadian case, McLean, J., said, that if the interest on the insurance would exceed the annual value of the testator's income while living and exercising his ordinary avocations, it would surely be competent for the company to show that the widow had sustained no pecuniary damages, and that only nominal damages should be given, if indeed any.[2] But, I should say that if the insurance went to some of the family only, the others would still have their right to substantial damages." [3]

"I believe," continued the irrepressible Jones, "that if an injured man settles with the company for a sum of money, that puts an end to the whole matter, and if he afterwards shuffles off this mortal coil nothing more is to be had."

"Yes; once and forever, is the rule, even if the unfortunate makes a mistake and takes too little." [4]

"Can you make money out of the slaughter of children?"

"Oh, certainly; though in England doubts have been suggested as to whether damages were obtainable to compensate for the loss of the services of a child so young as to be unable to earn

[1] Hicks *v.* Newport A. & H. Rw., mentioned in 4 B. & S. 403; see Bradburn *v.* G. W. Rw., L. R., 10 Ex. 3, where it was held that money received on an accident insurance policy could not be considered in reduction of damages for injuries caused by negligence.

[2] Ferrie *v.* Great Western Rw., 15 U. C. Q. B. 517.

[3] Pym *v.* Great Northern Rw., 4 B. & S. 397, Ex. Ch.

[4] Read *v.* Great Eastern Rw., L. R., 3 Q. B. 555; but see remark of Erle, C. J., in Pym *v.* Gt. N. Rw., 4 B. & S. 406; and Coleridge, J., in Blake *v.* Midland Rw., 18 Ad. & El. (N. S.), 93.

anything;[1] but in New York a mother recovered $1,300 for the death of a daughter seven years old."[2]

"That was a pretty good figure for a female youngster."

"Yes, as the pecuniary loss is not supposed to be extended beyond the minority of the child.[3] In England, however, a father recovered for the loss of a son twenty-seven years old, but unmarried, who had been accustomed to make occasional presents to his parents.[4] There the old man rather 'tried to stick it on'; he had a swell funeral and bought crape for the family and wanted the company to pay for them; the jury said 'Yea,' but the court said 'Nay.' In one case, however, a mourning husband recovered the funeral expenses of his wife.[5] As a rule, damages of a pecuniary nature must be shown; so, where a son was in the habit of assisting his father by carrying round coals for him, it was held that £75 was too much to give the old man for compensation for his death.[6] In an Irish case, where a boy of fourteen, earning no wages and whose business capabilities were valued at *six-pence* per day, was killed, it

1 Bramhall *v.* Lees, 29 Law Times, 111.

2 Court of Appeals, 14 N. Y. 310.

3 State *v.* Baltimore & Ohio Rw., 24 Md. 84; but see Penn. Rw. *v.* Adams, 55 Penn. St. 499.

4 Dalton *v.* S. E. Rw. 4 C. B. (N. S.), 296.

5 Redfield on Railways, vol. ii. p. 275.

6 Franklin *v.* S. E. Rw. 3 H. & N. 211; Duckworth *v.* Johnson, 4 H. & N. 653.

was considered that the probability of his assisting his mother was good evidence to go to the jury.[1]

"What sums have been given and allowed by the court for the death of the father?"

"Well, it was considered that $12,000 was not too much for the widow and three children of an industrious well-to-do farmer;[2] in an English case £1,000 was given to the widow, and £1,500 to each of eight young children, $65,000 in all;[3] then $1,300 for that baby girl.[4] But when $20,000 was given as damages for the death of a blacksmith — the inventor of a patent plough — who was killed at the celebrated Desjardins Canal accident, a new trial was granted, as the court thought the sum enormously excessive.[5] On the other hand, in one case, twelve miserable jurymen, who doubtless would have eagerly skinned a mosquito for the sake of its hide and tallow, gave £1 to a poor widow, and ten shillings each to her two fatherless children.[6] So you see the sum goes by the rule of thumb."

"So it appears," answered my young friend, who sucked in knowledge as a sponge does water — only to lose it again. "But some of those are not bad figures."

"Certainly not; yet they are by no means as

[1] Condon *v.* Great Southern & Western Rw., 16 Ir. C. L. R. 415.

[2] Secord *v.* Great Western Rw., 15 U. C. Q. B. 631.

[3] Pym *v.* Great Northern Rw., 4 B. & S. 397 Ex. Ch.

[4] Court of Appeals, 14 N. Y. 310.

[5] Morley *v.* Great Western Rw., 16 U. C. Q. B. 504.

[6] Springett *v.* Balls, 7 B. & S. 477.

good as some people have got and had the pleasure of spending themselves. In one case, a man received $6,000 for a broken leg, which got well in about eight months:[1] another got $24,700 (Canada money) for the loss of his leg."[2]

"What a leg that must have been — a match for Miss Kilmansegg's precious limb, which

'Was made in a comely mould,
Of gold, fine virgin glittering gold,
As solid as man could make it —
Solid in foot, and calf, and shank,
A prodigious sum of money it sank;
In fact, 't was a branch of the family bank,
And no easy matter to break it.

All sterling metal, — not half-and-half,
The goldsmith's mark was stamped on the calf, —
'Twas pure as from Mexican barter.

'T was a splendid, brilliant, beautiful leg,
Fit for the Court of Scander-Beg,
That precious leg of Miss Kilmansegg!'"

Exclaimed Tom Jones glowing with poetic fire, his eye in a fine frenzy rolling at the thought of the bawbees.

"Cease exhibiting your Hood," I said severely. "In another case $10,000 was obtained for something or other, when if the man had been killed outright his friends would only have got $5,000.[3] But in these three cases, new trials were granted, as will always be the way where the damages are

[1] Clapp v. Hudson R. R., 19 Barb. 461.
[2] Batchelor v. Buffalo & Brantford Rw., 5 U. C. C. P. 127.
[3] Collins v. Albany & Sch. Rw., 12 Barb. 492.

so excessive as to strike every one as beyond all measure unreasonable and corrupt, and as showing the jury to have been actuated by passion, corruption, or prejudice.[1] Where, however, a woman had lost one arm and the use of the other, and was so bruised, battered, blackened and injured that she was in constant pain, and her health and memory were impaired, and in three successive trials recovered $10,000, $18,000, and $22,250 respectively, the first two verdicts were set aside, but she was allowed to keep the third.[2] And where one was disabled for two years, $4,500 was held not exorbitant compensation;[3] and in Connecticut, $1,800 to a two year old baby for the loss of a leg and hand were given and retained.[4] And where a man broke his leg in two places, was confined to his room for four or five months during which time the injured leg became shorter than the other, he was allowed to retain $2,000 awarded to him by the jury,[5] and Mr. Rockwell, who had to keep his bed six weeks, suffering great pain the while, and could not attend to his business for several months and had to pay $1,500 to the disciples of Galen, was allowed to keep $12,000 given him by twelve jurymen.[6]

1 Coleman v. Southwick, 9 Johns. 45; Gilbert v. Burtenshawf, Cowp. 230; Hewlett v. Cruchley, 5 Taunt. 277.

2 Shaw v. Boston & Worcester Rw., 8 Gray, 45.

3 Curtiss v. Rochester & S. Rw., 20 Barb. 282.

4 Redfield on Railways, vol. ii., p. 243.

5 Fairbanks v. G. W. R., 35 Q. B. (Ont.), 523.

6 Rockwell v. Third Avenue Rw., 64 Barb. N. Y. 438.

But $5,000 for a damaged hand was held too much.[1] As these things rest a great deal in the discretion of the jury they must of necessity be more or less uncertain. But the amount paid by railway companies for compensation for injuries is enormous: the Revere accident, in Massachusetts, a few years ago, cost the company half a million of dollars, and in England between 1867 and 1871 the various companies paid out $10,000,000 for this purpose."

"Can you sue more than once?"

"No; you must go for all your damages, present and prospective, in one action."[2]

"What do you actually get paid for?"

"The effect of the accident — both at the present time and in the future — upon one's health, use of limbs, ability to attend to business and pursue the course of life that one otherwise would have done, the bodily pain and suffering endured, and in fact all injuries that are the legal, direct, and necessary results of the accident.[3] If sufficient time has not elapsed to enable the injury to be properly computed, the trial should be postponed.[4] A jury may be properly asked to consider the fact that the injured one had a reasonable prospect of increasing his income al-

[1] Union Pacific Rw. *v.* Hand, 7 Kan. 380.

[2] Hodsoll *v.* Stallebras, 11 Ad. & El. 301; Whitney *v.* Clarendon, 18 Vt. 252.

[3] Curtiss *v.* Rochester & S. Rw. 20 Barb. 282; Memphis, etc. Rw. *v.* Whitfield, 44 Miss. 466.

[4] Speers *v.* G. W. R., 5 Pr. Rep. (Ont.), 173.

though at the time it was small.[1] In some cases the plaintiff has been allowed to add to his actual damages of loss of time, expense of cure, pain and suffering, and prospective disability, if any — counsel fees not recoverable as taxable costs,[2] but this rule is not now followed.[3] A husband may recover for the expense of the cure of his wife, and for the loss of her services.[4] Expenses incurred by sickness of a wife caused by the death of her child,[5] and damages for premature labor, and birth of a still-born child caused by collision, are recoverable.[6] One young lady, who was seriously injured by the upsetting of a passenger car, sought to get additional damages because the prospects of her forming a matrimonial alliance were lessened by her injuries, but the poor thing failed in her attempt for lack of evidence on the point, and because her attorney had neglected to insert the special claim in the declaration." [7]

"Oh that was too bad," said Jones, "for the desire of marriage — her chances of which had been lessened — arises naturally from the principle of reproduction which stands next in impor-

[1] Fair *v.* L. & N. W. Rw., Q. B. 18 W. R. 66.

[2] Barnard *v.* Poor, 21 Pick. 381; Sandback *v.* Thomas, 1 Stark. 306.

[3] Grace *v.* Morgan, 2 Bing. (N. C.), 534; Jenkins *v.* Biddulph, 4 Bing. 160.

[4] Hopkins *v.* Atlantic & St. Lawrence Rw., 36 N. H. 9; Pack *v.* Mayor of New York, 3 Comst. 489; Campbell *v.* G. W. R., 20 U. C. C. P. 345.

[5] Ford *v.* Monroe, 20 Wendell, 210.

[6] Fitzpatrick *v.* Great Western Rw., 12 U. C. Q. B. 645.

[7] Hanover Rw. *v.* Coyle, 55 Penn. 396.

tance to its elder born correlative, self-preservation, and is equally a fundamental law of existence: it is the blessing which tempered with mercy the justice of the expulsion from Paradise; it was impressed upon the human creation by a benevolent Providence, to multiply the images of Himself, and so promote His own glory and the happiness of his creatures. Not man alone but the whole animal and vegetable kingdoms are under an imperious necessity to obey its mandates. From the lord of the forest to the monster of the deep; from the subtlety of the serpent to the innocence of the dove; from the celastic embrace of the mountain Kalima to the descending fructification of the lily of the plain, all nature bows submissively to this primeval law. Even the flowers which perfume the air with their fragrance and decorate the forests and the fields with their hues, are but curtains to the nuptial bed. The principles of morality, the policy of nations, the doctrines of the common law, the law of nature and the law of God, unite in condemning any act which hinders people entering into the holy estate of wedlock." [1]

"My conscience, Tom Jones, how did you become master of such mighty and glowing strains of high toned eloquence," I asked, as I "astonied stood and blank."

"Oh, I have an action for breach of promise

[1] Per Lewis, J. Commonwealth *v.* Stauffer, 10 Barr. 350.

coming on to-morrow, and I thought I would see if I knew the peroration of my address to the jury."

"Did you compose it?" I asked.

"Not quite. Mr. Justice Lewis, of Pennsylvania, originally uttered the words in giving judgment in a will case. Now then," said Jones, after a pause, "what about the employee that was killed."

"Ah! more of them are killed every year than the number of soldiers who died during the Ashantee war; 1,000 or 1,200 appears to be the annual number in the old country. But it is clearly settled both in England and America, that a servant who is injured through the negligence or misconduct of a fellow servant, can maintain no action against the master,[1] if the latter has taken due care not to expose him to unnecessary danger,[2] and has made a proper selection of servants — competent and trustworthy — and has a sufficient number of them,[3] and has himself not been guilty of negligence,[4] and takes care to furnish and maintain suitable and safe machinery and structures,[5] and if a servant continues his work

1 Priestley *v.* Fowler, 3 M. & W. 1; Farwell *v.* Boston & W. Rw., 4 Met. 49; Brown *v.* Maxwell, 6 Hill, N. Y. 592.

2 Hutchinson *v.* York, etc., Rw., 5 Ex. 353; Wiggett *v.* Fox, 11 Ex. 837; Keegan *v.* Western Rw., 4 Selden, 175.

3 Tarrant *v.* Webb, 18 C. B. 805; Frazier *v.* Penn. Rw., 38 Penn. St. 104; Wright *v.* New York Central, 28 Barb. 80; Hard *v.* Vermont & Canada Rw., 32 Vt. 473.

4 Ormond *v.* Holland, 1 El. Bl. & El. 102.

5 Bartonshill Coal Co. *v.* Reid, 3 Macq. H. L. Cas. 266; Tarrant *v.* Webb, 18 C. B. 797; Weems *v.* Mathieson, 4 Macq. 215.

knowing that his fellows are incompetent, or the machinery defective, he is guilty of contributory negligence." [1]

"It seems," remarked my friend, "strange that if my coachman runs over a stranger and kills him, I have to make reparation, but if he runs over the footman and disposes finally of that man of buttons, it is a matter of no importance. And in this case it will prove very hard on the poor family."

"Ah, well! judges and juries must not be drawn out of the path of duty even by their feelings for the widow and the orphan. The reason of the law is, that when a servant engages to serve a master he undertakes to run all the ordinary risks of the service, which includes, of course, the negligence of fellow servants acting in the discharge of their duty towards their common master.[2] If the rule was otherwise it might become very hard on the master; as Lord Abinger suggests, the footman who sits behind the carriage would have an action against his master if he came to grief through the negligence of the coachmaker or harness maker, or through the drunkenness, neglect, or want of skill of the coachee; in fact the poor master would be liable to his servant for the negligence of the chambermaid, in putting him into a bed with damp sheets, whereby he took

[1] Holmes v. Clark, 6 H. & N. 349; 7 Ibid. 937.
[2] Morgan v. Vale of Neath Rw., L. R., 1 Q. B. 149.

the rheumatism; for that of the upholsterer in sending him a crazy bedstead, whereby he fell down while asleep and injured himself; or for the negligence the cook in not properly cleaning the copper vessels used in the kitchen; of the butcher in supplying the family with meat injurious to health; of the builder for a defect in the foundation of the house whereby it fell, and injured both the master and the servants in its ruins." [1]

"But what is a fellow servant?"

"In England all the servants of the same person, or company, engaged in carrying forward the common enterprise — although in different departments, widely separated or strictly subordinated to others — are fellow servants and are bound to run the hazard of any negligence or wrong doing which may be committed by any of their number,[2] and it makes no difference that the negligence is imputed to a servant of superior authority, whose directions the other was bound to obey.[3] But in some of the American cases, it has been held that employees, who are so far removed from each other as that the one is bound to obey the other, are not fellow servants within the rule; [4] other judges, however, have denied

[1] Priestley *v.* Fowler, 3 M. & W. 1.

[2] Tunney *v.* Midland Rw., L. R., 1 C. P. 291; see also, Plant *v.* G. T. R.. 27 U. C. Q. B. 78.

[3] Feltham *v.* England, L. R., 2 Q. B. 33.

[4] Coon *v.* Syracuse & Utica Rw., 1 Selden, 492; Louisville & N. Rw. *v.* Collins, 5 Am. Law Reg. (N. S.), 265

this qualification;[1] and now it seems settled that it is sufficient to bring the case within the general rule, if the servants are employed in the same general service,[2] or under the same general control."[3]

"All this may be very true, but then you see, my dear Eldon, my man was killed in consequence of the state of the track," said Jones.

"Why in the name of all that is sacred and profane did you not remind me of that before. In one case a company was held responsible for an injury to one of its servants through the track being out of repair,[4] but in others it was considered that if the line was properly built and inspected it was all that could be required.[5] So you can draw your own conclusions, for I am getting tired of you."

"Well, I'm off, and am much obliged. But, oh, one point more before I leave you. One of the men was coming from Chicago and had a coupon ticket which he purchased at the station there, does that make any difference?"

"Through tickets do not import a contract with the purchaser on the part of the company selling

[1] Farwell *v.* Boston & W. Rw., 4 Met. 49, 60; Gillshannon *v.* Stony Brook Rw., 10 Cush. 228; Chicago & N. W. Rw. *v.* Jackson, 55 Ill. 492.

[2] Wright *v.* N. Y. C., 25 N. Y. 562; and see Baird *v.* Pettit, 29 Phil. Rep. 397.

[3] Abraham *v.* Reynolds, 5 H. & N. 142; Hard *v.* Vermont & Canada Rw., 32 Vt. 475.

[4] Snow *v.* Housatonic Rw., 8 Allen, 441.

[5] Faulkner *v.* Erie Rw., 49 Barb. 324; Warner *v.* Same, 8 Am. Law Reg. (N. S.), 209.

to carry him beyond the limits of their own line: the coupons are to be considered as so many distinct tickets for each road, sold by the first company as agent for the others;[1] and each successive company is responsible for all injuries to through passengers while upon its own line and in passing to the next company's line.[2] The companies cannot be considered partners so as to render each liable for injuries or losses occurring upon the whole route."[3]

"Is not that different from the rule as to carrying goods and baggage, and the rule in England?"

"As to carriers of goods or baggage taking pay and giving checks or tickets through, the first company is ordinarily liable for the entire route;[4] and in England it has been decided[5] that where a railway company contracts to carry a passenger from one terminus to another, and on the journey the train has to pass over the line of another railway company, the company issuing the ticket incurs the same responsibility as that other company, over whose line the train runs and by whose default the accident happens, would incur if the contract to carry had been entered into by them. The company issuing the ticket is liable for the negligence of the servants of any other company

[1] Sprague *v.* Smith, 29 Vt. 421; Hood *v.* N. Y. & N. H. Rw., 22 Conn. 1
[2] Knight *v.* P. S. & P. R. Rw., 56 Me. 234; 2 Redf. Am. Rw. cases, 458.
[3] Ellsworth *v.* Tartt, 26 Ala. 733.
[4] McCormick *v.* Hudson R. Rw., 4 E. D. Smith, 181.
[5] Great Western Rw. *v.* Blake, 7 H. & N. 987, Ex. Ch.

over whose line the passenger has to pass to reach his journey's end; the contract with the passenger being the same whether the journey be entirely over the line of the first company, or partly over that of another company, and whether the passage over the other line be under an agreement to share profits or simply under running powers; and that contract is, not only that they will not be themselves guilty of any negligence, but that due care will be used in carrying the passengers from one end of the journey to the other, so far as is within the compass of railway management.[1] In fact, the rule in regard to companies that run over other roads than their own seems now to be pretty well established; and it is, that the first company is responsible for the entire route and must take the risk of the employees of the other companies;[2] and where another company has running powers over the first company's line, the first company is not liable for any injury arising through the negligence of such other company; though if it were a case of goods they would be liable, because they are then insurers." [3]

"I suppose in England you can only sue the company granting the ticket."

"Yes. I would just add, so that you may have

[1] Thomas *v.* Rhymney Rw. Co., L. R., 6 Q. B. 266, Ex. Ch.; and John *v.* Bacon, L. R., 5 C. P. 437.

[2] Redfield on Railways, vol. ii. p. 303; Railway Co. *v.* Barron, 5 Wall, 90; Ayles *v.* S. E. Rw., L. R., 3 Ex. 146; Birkett *v.* Whitehaven Junction Rw., 4 H. & N. 730; Sprague *v.* Smith, 29 Verm. 421, was an exceptional case.

[3] Wright *v.* Midland Rw., L. R., 8 Ex. 137.

an exhaustive discourse on the subject, that if mischief arises from the act of a stranger in leaving a log of wood across the railway, or doing any other act which might endanger a railway train passing along the line of another company, an action cannot be maintained against the railway company, because in that case there would not be any direct or indirect breach of duty, or breach of contract, on their part; they would not be liable on their own line, or on any other company's line for that;[1] the same doctrine was held where a stranger had wilfully and maliciously placed a stone upon the track which threw off the train.[2] If, however, a man falls off the cars on to the track, because he has no proper place to sit and his body throws the train off, this will afford no excuse for damages to the man's luggage from such upsetting.[3] So, where the covetous greed of a young bullock induced him to force his way through a hedge to gain some tempting grass that grew luxuriantly on the track, and the collision with him of the train hurt Mr. Buxton who was on board; and it appeared that B. had been a passenger on the defendants' railway to be carried from Y. to T., and to reach T. it was necessary

[1] Mytton *v.* Midland Rw., 4 H. & N. 615; Great Western Rw., *v.* Blake, 7 H. & N. 987, Ex. Ch.; Weed *v.* Saratoga Rw., 19 Wend. 534.

[2] Latch *v.* Rimmer Rw., 27 L. J., Ex. 155; see also, Cunningham *v.* Grand Trunk Rw., 31 U. C. Q. B. 350; Curtis *v.* Rochester & Syracuse Rw., 18 N. Y. 534; Tennery *v.* Pippinger, 1 Phila. 543; Thayer *v.* St. Louis, A. & T. H. Rw. 22 Ind. 26; Pitts., Ft. Wayne, & Chicago Rw. *v.* Maurer, 21 Ohio, N. S. 421.

[3] Goldey *v.* Penn. Rw., 30 Penn. St. 242.

to travel over the line belonging to another company, and while journeying over the latter line the affair of the bullock took place. The court held that the contract having been made with the defendants they were the proper parties to be sued. A new trial was, however, granted because the judge had directed the jury that it was negligence in the defendants if the fences were insufficient; the court considering that there was no statutory obligation on the company, towards their passengers, to keep up the fences." [1]

"What would it have been if the bullock had jumped over the hedge instead of pushing through?" asked Jones.

"I don't understand." I returned.

"Why a case of cattle-lept-sy to be sure. Au revoir."

[1] Buxton *v.* Northeastern Rw., L. R., 3 Q. B. 549.

CHAPTER XV.

BAGGAGE AGAIN.

Epistolary Model. — Dog lost. — Quitting a Moving Car. — When Liability for Luggage commences. — Goods of Third Party. — Left in the Car. — Baggage lost. — English Rule. — Limited Liability. — Personal Luggage, what it is. — Watch — Rings. — Pistol. — Railroad Porter. — Hotel 'Bus. — Tools and Pocket Pistols. — Fiddles and Merchandise. — Farewell.

MY DEAR WIFE, —

Your letter announcing your safe arrival at M——, if, indeed, you can be said to have arrived safely, considering all that befell you, made me happy this A. M. The tale of your disasters was really quite amusing, and I have passed some of my lonely hours most agreeably considering the law on the various points.

So poor Fox is gone ; doubtless the mangled remains of that poor cur lie stark and cold upon the railway line, and crows are gathering in the leaden skies to assist at his funereal obsequies ; or, perchance, he may be gracing the board at some restaurant in the familiar form of sausages. You say it appears that he slipped his head through the noose of the string by which he was tied in the baggage car ; if this be so the baggage man might have seen that he was not securely fastened ; and it was his duty to lock him up, or otherwise keep him safely.[1] Make out your bill, dearest, we 'll make the company pay. At what figure do you value him? (I had, however, better add that in a late case where a dog was fastened in the ordinary way, and there was nothing to show that he was likely to escape, the carrier was held justified in trusting to the owner having properly secured the animal.)[2]

Poor Miss Smith ought to have been more careful when she would insist upon going into the car to bid you a last adieu, even though her young man was waiting for her. She most certainly should not have attempted to leave the carriage after it was in motion, and when the conductor warned her not. Even if the conductor was to blame in negligently starting the train without the usual premonitory screech, and the unnecessary jerk assisted in the catastrophe, the company was not responsible; her conduct was the mere outcome of that perverseness which is the characteristic trait of the feminine nature.[3]

You never told me that Eliza Jane had taken her trunk to the station some half dozen hours before the train was to start; it was rather verdant of her so to do. I presume the desire to have a quiet drive with her John was the motive. The loss of her finery will teach her a lesson; however,

[1] Stuart *v.* Crawley, 2 Stark, 324.
[2] Richardson *v.* Northeastern Rw., L. R., 7 C. P. 75, note.
[3] Lucas *v.* Taunton & New Bedford Rw., 6 Gray, 64.

it will not really matter, as she can recover the value of her "things," for the responsibility of the company as common carriers attaches as soon as their servants receive the baggage of the traveller at the proper place; and the giving of the check does not control the time of the responsibility attaching.[1] One is a passenger, and entitled to sue for damages sustained, the moment he mounts the bus (run by the company) on his way to the station.[2] But where an intending passenger, fifteen minutes before the train was to start, entered a car at the terminus, left his valise on a vacant seat and went out; and on his return shortly afterwards his baggage was gone; as he did not show that there was any one in charge of the train or any other passenger on board, the court would not hold the company liable.[3] The fact that you took and paid for her ticket will not prevent E. J. maintaining an action for her loss,[4] for it makes no difference whether a passenger pays her own fare, or some one else kindly does it for her.[5] In fact, if one is travelling on a free pass by which the company stipulates to be excused from all loss or damage, still they are responsible for the wilful or careless misconduct of their servants.[6]

[1] Camden & Amboy Rw. *v.* Belknap, 21 Wendell, 354; Hickox *v.* Naugatuck Rw., 31 Conn. 281.
[2] Buffet *v.* Troy Rw., 40 N. Y. 168.
[3] Kerr *v.* G. T. R., 24 C. P. (Ont.), 209.
[4] Marshall *v.* York, N., & B. Rw., 11 C. B., 655.
[5] Van Horn *v.* Kermit, 4 E. D. Smith, 453.
[6] Mobile & Ohio Rw. *v.* Hopkins, 41 Ala. 486.

But, unfortunately, I fear that you must quietly submit to the loss of those things of yours which she had in her trunk, for the contract to carry was with her alone; the company thought that the trunk contained her luggage; if they had been told that it was not they might have objected to carry, considering the Saratogas you had, not to speak of bandboxes, bundles, and parcels; and even if you had had no luggage yourself, it would have been all the same;[1] and as they were not Eliza Jane's I don't suppose she can sue for them either.

And so that pretty dressing-case which I gave you on that memorable day when we twain became one flesh, is gone! you say that you put it under your seat in the car, and that it must have been left there when the porter carried your traps to the cab at your journey's end; well, I cannot say that placing it where you did was a very wise thing, still as another lady who once did the same in England recovered the value of her dressing-case (although she failed to recover the case itself),[2] so doubtless if money will dry your tears for the loss of that memento of our wedding-day, you will be consoled. Probably the fact of your name and address not being on it will not affect your rights in the matter.[3] A railway company is liable for the loss of a passenger's luggage though

[1] Becher *v.* G. E. Rw., L. R., 5 Q. B. 241.

[2] Richards *v.* London, B., & S. C. Rw., 7 C. B. 839.

[3] Campbell *v.* Caledonian Rw., 14 Ct. of Sess. Cas. 2 Ser. 806; 1 S. M. & P. 742.

carried in the carriage in which he himself is travelling.[1] Very special circumstances, and circumstances leading irresistibly to the conclusion that the traveller takes such personal control and charge of his luggage as altogether to give up all hold upon the company, are required before a court will say that the company as common carriers are not liable in the event of a loss.[2] Even if luggage is never given to a railroad servant but kept by the passenger in his own possession, still in the eye of the law it is considered to be in the custody of the company, so as to render them responsible for the loss.[3] In England, a railway company that receives goods or luggage, and books it for a certain place beyond the terminus of its road (unless it specially stipulates to be exempt for whatever happens on other lines), is responsible for any evil that befalls it before its arrival at its journey's end, even though it happens while the goods are passing over the rails of another company;[4] in fact one has no remedy except against the company with whom the contract is made. But the justice and soundness of the English decisions have been seriously questioned by

[1] Le Conteur *v.* London & S. W. Rw., L. R., 1 Q. B. 54.

[2] Ibid.

[3] Great Northern Rw. *v.* Shepherd, 8 Ex. 30; but see Tower *v.* Utica & Sch. Rw., 7 Hill, N. Y. 47.

[4] Muschamp *v.* Lancaster & Preston Junction Rw., 8 M. & W. 421; Watson *v.* Ambergate, N. & B. Rw., 15 Jur. 448; Bristol & Ex. Rw. *v.* Collins, 7 House Lords Cas. 194. The same rule applies in Canada, Smith *v.* G. T. Rw. 35 U. C. Q. B. 547.

the American courts, who think that the carrier is only liable for the extent of his own route, and for safe storage, and safe delivery to the next carrier.[1] Many cases, however, follow the English ones, and others hold that the responsibility is only *primâ facie*, and may be controlled by general usage among carriers, whether such usage be known to the traveller or not.[2] (But this subject is so mixed that I will show you what Judge Redfield says when you get back again.)[3] Where different railways — forming a continuous line — run their cars over the whole line and sell tickets for the whole route, checking baggage through, an action lies against any company for the loss of baggage.[4]

Of course if there was any notice on your ticket limiting the liability of the company with regard to your traps, you are bound thereby, even if you never read it;[5] for railway companies, as well as other carriers, may limit their responsibility by special contract of which notice is given to the passenger or owner, and to which he assents or does not object, subject to such exception, limitation, or qualification as reason and jus-

1 Farmers' & Mechanics' Bank *v.* Champlain Trans. Co., 16 Vt. 52; 18 Vt. 131; 23 Vt. 186; Van Santvoord *v.* St. John, 6 Hill, N. Y. 158.

2 Southern Express Co. *v.* Shea, 38 Ga. 519; Cincinnati, etc., Rw. *v.* Pontius, 19 Ohio (N. S.), 221.

3 Redfield on Railways, vol. ii., p. 126, *et seq.*

4 Hart *v.* Rensselaer & Saratoga Rw., 4 Seld. 37.

5 Zunz *v.* South-eastern Rw., L. R., 4 Q. B. 539; but see Kent *v.* Midland Rw. Co., L. R., 10 Q. B. 1; Henderson *v.* Stevenson, L. R., 2 S. & D. 470.

tice may require and a judge and jury decide with reference to each particular case.[1]

I don't exactly know what you had in that dressing-case of yours, but the rule is, "that whatever a passenger takes with him for his own personal care and convenience, or even for his instruction and amusement,[2] according to the habits or wants of the particular class to which he belongs, either with reference to the immediate necessities or the ultimate purpose of the journey, must be considered as personal luggage," for the loss of which the carrier is liable; [3] and articles of jewelry, such as a lady usually wears, are considered personal luggage.[4] So is a watch; [5] though in Tennessee a watch was not deemed a proper part of necessary baggage.[6] Where was yours? So are finger rings.[7] In one case a man was allowed to have two gold chains, two gold rings, a locket and a silver pencil-case; [8] so I will leave you to calculate how many a lady should be

[1] Carr *v.* Lancashire & York Rw., 7 Ex. 707; Redfield on Railways, vol. ii., p. 101. Where the condition on ticket was "that the company does not hold itself responsible for any delay, detention, or other loss arising off its lines," and the baggage was never delivered to any other company, held that meaning of last words was "out of the custody of the company." Kent *v.* Midland Rw., L. R., 10 Q. B. 1.

[2] Hawkins *v.* Hoffman, 6 Hill, 586.

[3] Cockburn, C. J., in Macrow *v.* Great Western Rw., L. R., 6 Q. B. 622; Great Northern Rw. *v.* Shepherd, 8 Ex. 38.

[4] Brooke *v.* Pickwick, 4 Bing. 218; McGill *v.* Rowand, 3 Penn. St. 451.

[5] Jones *v.* Voorhees, 10 Ohio, 145; Miss. C. Rw. *v.* Kennedy, 41 Miss. 471.

[6] Bomer *v.* Maxwell, 9 Humphrey, 621.

[7] McCormick *v.* Hudson River Rw., 4 E. D. Smith, 181.

[8] Bruty *v.* Grand Trunk Rw., 32 U. C. Q. B. 66.

allowed to carry about with her. Your swell gold spectacles would also come within the category;[1] and by the way, that linen which you bought for my new shirt fronts would be included[2] (if you were good enough to take it with you to make them up, and unfortunate enough to lose it); and that little present you were taking for your sister — perhaps.[3] I don't know what else you had in that case which will now know its place on our dressing table no more forever. Of course, your brushes, razors — *pardonnez moi, madame*, I forgot to whom I was writing — pen and ink, etc., are fairly baggage within the meaning of the term.[4]

Not content with the abandoment of your dressing-case, you say you lost a bandbox by stupidly letting a porter carry it for you to a cab, which you could not afterwards find: well, if it is the custom on that line for the company's porters to assist passengers to obtain cabs, within the station grounds, and place their baggage therein, the company will be liable for this loss also. This my old friend Butcher satisfactorily established: he had a carpet-bag with him containing a large sum of money, and this he wisely kept in his own possession while journeying up to London. On

1 *Re* H. M. Wright, Newberry Admiralty, 494.

2 Duffy *v.* Thompson, 4 E. D. Smith, 178.

3 Great Western Rw. *v.* Shepherd, 8 Ex. 38; but see Bell *v.* Drew, 4 E. D. Smith, 59.

4 Hawkins *v.* Hoffman, 6 Hill, N. Y. Rep. 589.

arriving at the station there, however, he unwisely — even Jove sometimes nods — let a porter take it from him for the purpose of securing a cab. The porter put the bag in a fly and then returned to the platform to get my friend's other luggage. Meanwhile cabby disappeared and the bag and all that was therein was lost. The court considered the company liable, as there had been a delivery of the bag to them to be carried, and no re-delivery to Butcher.[1] Where baggage has been lost, the owner may recover all reasonable expenses incurred in his hunt after it, such as telegraphing, cab-hire, etc.: but his loss of time is a dead loss.[2]

Your next misfortune was the loss of that new book I gave you, wherewith to beguile the weariness of the way; you say you left it in the omnibus that took you up to the hotel; well, omnibus drivers who take passengers from the stations about the towns are unquestionably responsible as common carriers.[3] Although in England it has been held that a cab-driver or hackney-coachman was not;[4] still they are bound to use an ordinary degree of care. If the hotel proprietor undertakes to provide free transit to and from the cars, and you lost your book in his 'bus, he is liable.[5]

[1] Butcher *v.* London & S. W. Rw., 16 C. B. 13.
[2] Morrison *v.* E. & N. A. Rw., 2 Pugsley's Rep. No. 3, p. 295.
[3] Peixotti *v.* McLaughlin, 1 Strob. 468.
[4] Brind *v.* Dale, 8 C. & P. 207; Ross *v.* Hill, 2 C. B. 887.
[5] Dickinson *v.* Winchester, 4 Cush. 115.

Although it deeply pains me to find the slightest fault with my spouse, still I must say that I think that you have been a little careless during this trip; in fact you have shown that the character your mother gave you was not quite a libel, when she said that you would lose your head were it not securely fastened on, and your tongue were it not in incessant use.

While I am writing to you in this strain, I may as well give you a little further information concerning what you may, and what you may not, carry as personal baggage; though doubtless you will soon forget all that I say, or if not, — at all events, — will not heed it, such is the forgetfulness and perverseness of that sex whose love, as Prince Charles Edward said, "is writ on water, whose faith is traced on sand."

Besides what I have already mentioned, if you are a sportsman you may take a gun, if a disciple of the gentle Izaak Walton, the necessary *instrumenta bella;*[1] if you are a joiner — I don't mean a parson — you may take a reasonable amount of tools with your clothes,[2] although perhaps you can't;[3] for in Pennsylvania a carpenter was permitted to carry a reasonable amount of his tools with him,[2] while in Ontario a brother of the same craft was not;[3] the judge thinking that a black-

[1] Macrow *v.* Great Western Rw., L. R., 6 Q. B 622; Hawkins *v.* Hoffman, 6 Hill, N. Y. Rep. 589.

[2] Porter *v.* Hildebrand, 14 Penn. St. 129.

[3] Bruty *v.* Grand Trunk Rw., 32 U. C. Q. B. 66.

smith might just as reasonably expect to carry his forge, or a farmer his plough, as part of his baggage. You may take new clothing and materials for yourself and family, though not for others; [1] if you are of a nervous disposition and desire to defend yourself against thieves and robbers, you may take a pocket pistol, — don't suppose I mean a brandy flask, — if you are a bellicose man of honor a couple of duelling pistols will be allowed,[2] or even a gun,[3] although in Maryland, one was not allowed to take a colt.[4] A theatre goer may take an opera glass; [5] a student on his way to college, manuscripts necessary for the prosecution of his studies; [6] but an artist cannot carry his pencil sketches as luggage in England; [7] although Cockburn, C. J., thought he could, and his easel as well.[8] J. Wilson, in a Canadian case, thought that one musically inclined might take a concertina, or a flute, or that instrument in the playing of which a western writer says "the resined hair of the noble horse travels merrily over the intestines of the agile cat;"[9] but fortunately for mankind in general the majority of the court held otherwise.

[1] Dexter *v.* S. B. & N. Y. Rw., 42 N. Y. 326.

[2] Woods *v.* Devon, 13 Ill. 746; Bruty *v.* G. T. Rw. 32 U. C. Q. B. 66.

[3] Davis *v.* Cayuga & S. Rw., 10 How. Prac. 330.

[4] Giles *v.* Fauntleroy, 13 Md. 126.

[5] Toledo & Wabash Rw. *v.* Hammond, 33 Ind. 379.

[6] Hopkins *v.* Westcott, 7 Am. Law Reg. (N. S.), 533.

[7] Mytton *v.* Midland Rw., 4 H. & N. 615; Morritt *v.* N. E. R., L. R., 1 Q. B. D. 302.

[8] Macrow *v.* Great Western Rw., L. R., 6 Q. B. 622.

[9] Bruty *v.* Grand Trunk Rw., 32 U. C. Q. B. 66.

You cannot carry merchandise, either in England,[1] the United States,[2] or the Dominion of Canada,[3] unless, indeed, it is carried openly, or so packed that the carrier can see what it is and does not object to it; nor samples, if you belong to the confraternity of commercial travellers;[4] nor can a banker take money as such;[5] nor can one carry silver spoons, nor surgical instruments, unless he is a disciple of Galen and Hippocrates;[6] nor boxes of jewelry for sale;[7] nor silver-ware;[8] nor the regalia and jewels of a society;[9] nor a sewing-machine;[10] and it is beyond a peradventure that if a carrier accepts a trunk, or baggage, containing such tabooed articles, without knowledge of such contents, he incurs no liability.[7] If he is deceived into taking it, he is not bound to carry it safely.[11]

But really, my dear, I must draw these remarks to a close, as the parsons say in their sermons. You cannot complain that this letter is

1 Great Western Rw. *v.* Shepherd, 8 Ex. 30; Macrow *v.* Great Western Rw., L. R., 6 Q. B. 616.

2 Pardee *v.* Drew, 25 Wend. 459; Collins *v.* Boston & Maine Rw., 10 Cush. 506.

3 Shaw *v.* Grand Trunk Rw., 7 U. C. C. P. 493.

4 Cahill *v.* London & N. W. Rw., 13 C. B. (N. S.), 818; Belfast B. L. & C. Rw. *v.* Keys, 9 House Lords Cas. 556; Hawkins *v.* Hoffman, 6 Hill, 586; Dibble *v.* Brown, 12 Ga. 217.

5 Phelps *v.* London & N. W. Rw., 19 C. B. (N. S.), 321.

6 Giles *v.* Fauntleroy, 13 Md. 126.

7 Richards *v.* Wescott, 2 Bosw. 589.

8 Bell *v.* Drew, 4 E. D. Smith, 59.

9 Nevins *v.* Bay State S. B. Co., 4 Bosw. 225.

10 Bruty *v.* Grand Trunk Rw., 32 U. C. Q. B. 66.

11 Sleat *v.* Fagg, 5 B. & Al. 342.

too short. There are several items of news — of babies born, brides be-wed, bodies buried, — and such like trivialities, of which I might have told you; but as you spoke about your losses I concluded that I would send you an instructive note, and let vain trifles rest quiescent until your return.

Though you may think that this epistle smacks somewhat of business, yet please reflect that you are my sleeping partner, and spend the greater portion of the profits of my office, and so 'tis becoming that you should be slightly acquainted with legal matters, especially as you are the daughter of my mother-in-law.

Adu! adu! O reservoir!

Your

SPANISH GRANDEE.

CHAPTER XVI.

TELEGRAMS AND FIRE.

Assault. — Authority of Officials. — A dear Kiss. — Arresting Passengers. — Telegraphic Messages. — Interesting Examples. — Who can sue for Mistake. — Fire-fiend's Pranks. — Train Arrives. — Liability Ceases. — Trunks in Warehouse. — Baggage left at Station. — Dissolving Domestic View.

WHEN the day arrived on which my wife was to return to me, I determined to go and meet her at N., so as to be on the spot to keep an eye on her baggage when she reached the station and avoid further loss and accident.

I bought my ticket and got into the proper car, but just as the train was on the point of starting I asked the porter if I was in the right carriage, he replied, I was not, and must get out; I hesitated, as the train was in motion, so he caught hold of me and violently pulled me out. We fell on the platform and I was considerably hurt, and what was as bad, the cars went on and left me behind. I went in search of the general superintendent of the line, as I was determined to seek redress, for a person who puts another in his place to do a class of acts in his absence necessarily leaves him to determine, according to the circumstances which arise, when an act of that class is to be done; consequently he is answerable for the wrong of the person so intrusted, either in the manner of doing such an act, or in doing such an act under circumstances in which it ought not to have been done; provided that what is done is not done from any caprice of the servant, but in the course of the employment.[1] And in a similar case it was held that the act of the porter, in pulling a man out of the carriage, was an act done within the course of his employment as the company's servant, and one for which they were therefore responsible.[2]

Railway companies are liable for all the acts of their servants and agents committed in the discharge of their business and their employment, within the range of such employment, whether wilful or negligent.[3] The injured person has to show that his assailant was not only a servant of the company, but that he had authority so to treat him, or that such conduct was subsequently ratified by the company.[4] Where a conductor chancing to be alone in the car with Miss Cracker, cracked some jokes, sat down beside her, put his hand in her muff with her's (although she objected that there was no room for it), threw

[1] Bayley *v.* Manchester, etc., Rw., L. R., 7 C. P. 415.

[2] Ibid.

[3] Phil. & R. Rw. *v.* Derby, 14 How. 468; Noyes *v.* Rutland, etc., Rw., 27 Vt. 110; Yarborough *v.* Bank of England, 16 East. 6

[4] Roe *v.* Berkenhead & L. Rw., 7 W. H. & G. 36.

his arms around her neck, and kissed her five or six times, while she struggled to escape. Miss C. to have sweet revenge, the kisses being so sour, and not relishing such blandishments and disliking chaps about her lips, or a railway man's bill stuck in her face, had him arrested and fined $25 for an assault: the company then dismissed the gay Lothario from their employ, and were rather surprised when the injured female sued them and recovered against them $1,000. The court considered the verdict was not excessive, and that a carrier's contract bound him to protect his passengers against all the world, which in this case had not been done. It was not denied that if such an attack had been made by a stranger and the conductor had neglected to protect Miss C. the company would have been liable, but it was contended that the company was not responsible for the malicious breach of the contract by their servant, the conductor. Ryan, C. J., thought such a contention was much like saying that if one hired a dog to guard sheep against wolves, and the dog slept while a wolf made away with a sheep, the owner of the dog would be liable ; but if the dog played wolf, and devoured the sheep himself, the owner would not be liable. Every woman has a right to assume that when she travels in a car she will meet nothing, see nothing, hear nothing, to wound her delicacy, or insult her womanhood.[1]

[1] Craker *v.* Chicago & N. W. Rw., 36 Wis. 657.

Some courts have held that a railway company can only act through their officers and servants, and as they, of necessity, commit their trains absolutely to the charge of men of their own appointment, and passengers of necessity commit to them their safety and comfort while journeying, the whole power and authority of the company for that purpose is vested on those officers; and as far as travellers are concerned they are to be considered as the corporation itself; and the latter is as responsible for the acts of the officers in running the train towards the passengers in it, as the officers would be for themselves were they the proprietors of the road and train.[1] Exemplary damages, however, will not be given against a company for the malicious acts of its agent, unless it is shown that the company expressly authorized or confirmed the deeds.[2]

A railway is supposed to have at its stations officers with authority to do all such things as are necessary and expedient for the protection of the company's property and interests, and for the apprehension of wrong-doers; and where there are persons present who are acting as if they had express authority, it is *primâ facie* evidence that they had such authority,[3] and the company will

[1] Bass *v.* Chicago & N. W. Rw., 36 Wis. 450; Craker *v.* C. & N. W. Rw., 33 Wis. 657; Goddard *v.* G. T. R , 57 Me. 202.

[2] M. & M. R. R. Co. *v.* Finney, 10 Wis. 388; but see Goddard *v.* G. T. R., 57 Me. 202; Sanford *v.* Rw. Co., 23 N. Y. 343.

[3] Goff *v.* Gt. Northern Rw., 3 E. & E. 672.

be answerable if their officers, in the exercise of their discretion, make a mistake and apprehend an innocent person, or commit an assault through an excess of duty, or do any other act that cannot be justified.[1] And it makes no difference with regard to the responsibility of the company that the servant disobeyed the directions of his superiors, if he was acting within the scope of his employment at the time.[2] But when he does an act which he has no authority to do, the company are not liable;[3] nor are they when he does an act which the company themselves have no authority to do.[4] And thus a seeming paradox arose in one case where a station master arrested a man for not paying the fare of a horse he had with him, and it was held that (as the company itself could not have done so) the company were not liable, though had the zealous official arrested him for not paying his own fare, damages might have been recovered against the company.[5]

Thus ruminating over my wrongs and chewing the bitter cud of hatred and malice, I found my way into the office of the chief official, but as that important functionary was *non est*, I had to nurse my wrath until some more convenient season.

Just then a friend came up and showed me a

[1] Giles *v.* Taff Vale Rw., 2 E. & B. 822; Moore *v.* Metropolitan Rw., L. R., 8 Q. B. 36.

[2] Phil. & Read. Rw. *v.* Derby, 14 How. (U. S.), 468.

[3] Edwards *v.* London & N. W. Rw., L. R., 5 C. P. 445.

[4] Poulton v. London & S. W. Rw., L. R., 2 Q. B. 534.

[5] Ibid.

telegram which seemed perfectly enigmatical and worthy of the Sphinx of yore, and we thus got speaking concerning such messages (or as they are often rightly called tell-o-crams). He asked me if I had ever noticed the case where a gentleman telegraphed for *two hand* bouquets, and the operator changed *hand* into *hund* and added *red*, making the order for " Two hundred bouquets." The florist delighted at the extensive order, procured a quantity of expensive flowers, which the other party of course refused to accept, so the poor flower-man had to sue the company for damages, which he recovered,[1] as well on the ground of breach of contract, as of breach of duty, the telegraph company being public servants.

" I believe that where the company give notice that they will not be responsible except for repeated messages, such a condition will be held good," I said.

" Yes.[2] There have been several cases showing the damage which the company will have to pay for mistakes in the performance of their duty : in one where a merchant sent the message ' Stop sewing pedal braid till I see you,' and it was delivered ' Keep sewing, etc., etc.,' and in consequence a large quantity of unfashionable braid was manufactured which the merchant received and disposed of in the best manner. He was

1 N. Y. & Wash. Print. Tel. Co. *v.* Dryburgh, 35 Penn. St. 298.

2 McAndrew *v.* Electric Tel. Co., 17 C. B. 3; Wann *v.* Western, etc., Tel. Co., 37 Mo. 472.

held entitled to recover the whole loss sustained in consequence of the error;[1] and it was so held where the message was changed from '5,000 sacks of salt,' into 5,000 casks:[2] the fact that the error was made in the transmission because the message was unintelligible to the operator will not excuse the company, so long as the words were plain."[2]

"How is the law in England?"

"It has been held there, and in Canada, that the party employing the telegraph company, or sending the message on his own account, is the only party who can maintain an action for any failure to perform their duty in respect of the message.[3] And where a message was sent for *three rifles* and when received it read *the rifles*, and the plaintiff supposing it referred to a former communication sent the sender of the despatch fifty rifles, the number before named; and these were refused; the plaintiff sued the sender for the price, but the court held that the defendant was not responsible for the mistake in transmitting the message, and that the plaintiff could only recover for three rifles.[4] The American jurists think that the English courts are guilty of an inconsistency, if not of a blunder, in holding that the only party who can sue the company is not re-

[1] Lockwood *v.* Ind. Line of Tel. Co., N. Y., C. P. 1865.

[2] Rittenhouse *v.* The same, 1 Daly, C. P. 474.

[3] Playford *v.* United Kingdom Tel. Co., L. R., 4 Q. B. 706; Feaver *v.* Montreal Tel. Co., 23 U. C. C. P. 150.

[4] Henkel *v.* Pape, L. R., 6 Ex. 7.

sponsible for the mistake. They say that the party who suffers by the mistake should, at all events, be allowed to maintain an action to recover the damage sustained by him; and they say that is the rule throughout the republic.[1] In an action against the company that delivers the message, where it has passed over several lines, they may excuse themselves by showing that the negligence complained of was that of some prior line.[2] Where there are several connected lines the company that took the message are generally liable for any negligence or mistake in the transmission."[3]

"It seems to be the law that the regulations of a telegraph company relieving them from liability, unless the message is repeated, are reasonable, and will free them from the effects of many mistakes;[4] but they will not be construed so as to release the company from liability occasioned by their own wilful misconduct or negligence,[5] as where *our* was changed into *your*,[6] or the message was never sent,[7] or delayed in delivery;[8] there

[1] Redfield on Railways, vol. ii., p. 314.

[2] La Grange *v.* S. W. Tel. Co., 25 La. An. 383.

[3] De Rutte *v.* Tel. Co., 1 Daly, 547.

[4] McAndrew *v.* Electric Tel. Co., 17 C. B. 3; but see Tyler *v.* W. U. Tel. Co., 5 Chi. Leg. News, 550; Wolf *v.* W. Tel. Co., 62 Pa. St. 83.

[5] N. Y. & Wash. Tel. Co. *v.* Dryburgh, 35 Penn. St. 298; True *v.* International Tel. Co., 60 Maine, 9; Sweetland *v.* Illinois, etc., Tel. Co., 27 Iowa, 433.

[6] Sellers *v.* W. U. Tel. Co., 3 Am. Law Reg. 777.

[7] Birney *v.* N. Y. & Wash. Tel. Co., 18 Maryland, 341.

[8] U. S. Tel. Co. *v.* Gildersleeve, 29 Maryland, 232; Bryant *v.* Am. Tel. Co., 1 Daly, 575.

must, however, be proof of negligence distinct from the infirmities of telegraphing.[1] Some of the American courts, however, have held that the receiver of the message is not bound by such a notice.[2] The company may restrict their liability on other points as well, by giving notice; but the restriction must be reasonable, not one, for instance, that the company would not be responsible for mistakes to an amount greater than that paid for the message.[3] The notice will, moreover, only benefit the company to which it is confined by the contract, and not a connecting line.[4]

"But suppose one is not aware of these rules and regulations?"

"To prevent one recovering they must be brought home to his knowledge[5] but he will be presumed to know what is on the blank used, and to make the conditions thereon his own, whether he read them or not."[6]

"Speaking about the freaks of the telegraph, did you see that one about the young parson who was about to start for his new parish, but was unexpectedly delayed by the inability of the Presbytery to ordain him? To explain his non-arrival he

1 Ellis *v.* Am. Tel. Co., 13 Allen, 226; and Wann *v.* West. U. Tel. Co., 37 Mo. 472.

2 La Grange *v.* S. W. Tel. Co., 25 La. An. 385.

3 True *v.* International Tel. Co., 60 Maine, 9.

4 Squire *v.* W. U. Tel. Co., 98 Mass. 232.

5 Camp *v.* West. Union Tel. Co., 1 Met. (Ky.) 164.

6 West. Union Tel. Co. *v.* Carew, 15 Mich. 525; Wolf *v.* W. Tel. Co., 62 Pa. St. 83; but see Henderson *v.* Stevenson, L. R., 2 S. & D. 470.

telegraphed to the church officials, 'Presbytery lacked a quorum to ordain.' In the course of its journey this got strangely metamorphosed, and the message-boy handed to the astonished deacons a telegram saying, "Presbytery tacked a worm on to Adam." The sober elders were sorely discomposed and mystified, but after grave consultation the happy thought struck one of them that this was the new minister's facetious way of announcing his marriage, and accordingly they provided lodgings for two instead of one."

"That is rather rich."

Thus chatting with my friend about the telegraph, the law and the profits thereof, occasionally indulging in the luxury of that odious weed of the great Sir Walter Raleigh, and frequently practising the bibulistic art, the time passed rapidly and pleasantly enough, and at length the shrill ear-piercing screech of a locomotive announced the arrival of the train, containing, as Horace neatly puts it, *animæ dimidium meæ*, or as ordinary folks say, "my better half." After the usual osculatory exercises, I inspected the amount of her handboxes, bundles, satchels and checks, and concluded that it would be useless to expect a cabby to carry home such a vast amount of baggage, and at well nigh the noon of night it would be equally vain to endeavor to obtain the services of a carter; so, knowing that travellers have a reasonable time to claim and remove their baggage, I determined to leave it at the station for the night.

With the checks clinking together in my pocket and my wife by my side, and Eliza Jane in front of me, I drove home comfortably, thinking that in the morning the checks would bring forth the trunks; but alas! I leant upon a broken reed, and ere the morrow's light appeared the baggage and my right to recover for its loss had vanished for ever and ever, like a morning mist before the rising sun.

A fire broke out at the station and favored by the winds of heaven it grew into a mighty conflagration, and before the morning watch the devouring element had consumed the station and all that therein was.

After a visit to the charred and smouldering ruins of the once handsome depot — my numerous inquiries having confirmed my worst fears as to the total loss of my wife's apparel — I returned to my office to consult the law on the subject, before I encountered her ladyship with the direful news of the antics of the Fire Fiend. There I quickly found that after a reasonable time and opportunity to take away his baggage has been given to a traveller, the company's responsibility as carriers ends: they are no longer responsible for its absolute security, but degenerate into mere warehousemen bound to exercise only that care which a prudent man ordinarily does in keeping his own goods of a similar kind and value;[1] and that care is exercised by the company placing the goods in a secure warehouse;[2] or, as a Canadian Chief Justice of high repute and great experience says, "the terminus of the transport being reached, the duty of the common carrier is fulfilled by placing the goods in a safe place, alike safe from the weather and from danger of loss or theft."[3] It was perfectly clear that the company was not responsible to me for the loss of my baggage,[4] through the foul pranks of the Fire Fiend. And it would have been just the same if it had been stolen from the warehouse;[5] or if on the arrival of the train I had taken possession of the trunks, and afterwards for my own convenience handed them back to the baggage-master at the station to be kept until sent for, and they had come to grief or been pilfered;[6] unless, indeed, there was some gross negligence on the part of the company. And I found by my books that it is the duty of the company to have the baggage ready for delivery, upon the platform, at the usual place, until the owner may with due diligence call for, and receive

[1] Shepherd *v.* Bristol & Ex. Rw., L. R., 3 Ex. 189; Mote *v.* Chicago & N. W. Rw., 1 Am. Rep. 212; 27 Iowa, 22; Burnell *v.* N. Y. C., 45 N. Y. 187; Rock Island & Pacific Rw. *v.* Fairclough, 52 Ill. 106.

[2] Bartholemew *v.* St. Louis, Jacksonville, etc., Rw., 53 Ill. 227.

[3] Inman *v.* Buffalo &.L. H. Rw., 7 U. C. C. P. 325; O'Neill *v.* Great Western Rw., Ibid. 203; Bowie *v.* Buffalo, Brantford, & G. Rw., Ibid. 191.

[4] Roth *v.* Buffalo & State Line Rw., 34 N. Y. 548.

[5] Penton *v.* Grand Trunk Rw., 28 U. C. Q. B. 367; Campbell *v.* The same, Hilary Term, 1873 (Ont.).

[6] Minor *v.* Chicago & North Western Rw., 19 Wis. 40.

it; and that it is the owner's duty to call for and remove it within a reasonable time; and that "reasonable time" is directly upon the arrival of the train, making a reasonable allowance for delay caused by the crowded state of the depot at the time; but that the lateness of the hour makes no difference if the baggage be put upon the platform.[1] Nor does the fact of it being Sunday make any difference.[2] But if the traveller does not choose to call and take away his *impedimenta* (as Julius Cæsar calls it), the company do all they need by putting it into their baggage room and keeping it for him, with the liability of ordinary warehousemen.

Thus conscious that I should wring nothing from the iron grasp of the railway company, and that out of my own professional earnings I should have to replenish my wife's wardrobe, I went home sad, down-cast and dejected, to break the direful news to her.

Scarcely had I entered my house, which had been so peaceful and calm during the past few weeks, when my *alter ego* flew at me with a perfect storm of words and questionings as to why her trunks had not yet come up, and assertions that she had literally nothing to wear. (Though to the eyes of an ordinary mortal she appeared far from being *in puris naturalibus.*)

[1] Ouimit *v.* Henshaw, 35 Vt. 605.
[2] Jones *v.* Norwich & N. Y. T. Co., 50 Barb. 193.

When I told of the fate that had befallen her paraphernalia the storm increased into a hurricane, and when it was announced that the company were not liable, a perfect tornado — a cyclone — a typhoon — a simoon — of words, whirled with terrific fury around my head, then a perfect waterspout shot forth; and I, remembering suddenly an appointment down town, vanished from the scenes, resolved that henceforth both myself and my amiable — but hysterical — spouse would eschew the iron horse and his train forever, and living peaceable at home avoid the Wrongs and Rights of Travellers by Rail, by Stage, by Private Conveyance.

INDEX.

A.

C.

D.

R.

S.

T.

U.

V.

W.

www.ingramcontent.com/pod-product-compliance
Lightning Source LLC
LaVergne TN
LVHW010227110826
845151LV00004B/1215

* 9 7 8 1 4 2 5 5 2 6 1 7 7 *